Allison

Congratulations on your
marriage! I am/was honored
to be your officiant. I love
our many connections over
the years. Happy life, dear
ones and blessings always.

Fondly,
Rev. Michele / jle

My Journey of

55 Septembers

A
Teacher's
Story

Michele Hile

My Journey of 55 Septembers ~
A Teacher's Story

Self-Published:
Michele Hile
Straw Walker Ink, LLC
cen55375@centurytel.net
989-673-4332

Lay-out and Design:
Julie Purdy
Purdyville Publishing, LLC
julie@purdyvillepublishing.com

Edited:
Janis Stein
Stein Expressions, LLC
www.steinexpressions.com
and
Jenny (Klee) Emming
Jenny's Office Solutions, LLC

Printed:
BookMobile
5120 Cedar Lake Road
Minneapolis, MN 55416-1641

First Edition

ISBN - 978-0-615-72829-2

Dedication

I dedicate this book to my family.

First of all, to my mother, Irene Keene Kosa Churchill Capling, who recognized the value of an education, which she was denied, and relentlessly held that hope and vision for me.

To my husband, Tom, for always encouraging and supporting me in my dreams.

To my sons, John and Allen, from whom I have learned life's most important lessons. They have been wonderful teachers to me.

Acknowledgments

To Barbara Ruckle, my dear friend and teaching partner for thirty-four of my thirty-eight years, next door neighbor in farm country, and mother of three sons similar in ages to my two boys. Thank you for tirelessly suggesting, sometimes demanding, that I write a book. You did such a good job convincing me that I needed to write a book that it became part of the reason I retired, leaving our thirty-four-year partnership.

To my dear friend, Kay Montei, for believing I had the ability to write a book someone might want to read. Thank you for your confidence.

To Rhonda Bringard, for asking that fateful fall day if I would be your mentor, since another teacher had retired the previous June. Thank you for thinking that I had something of value to offer.

To my "publishing team," Janis Stein, my editor, not only for your editing but for your meticulous guidance and kind patience as you shared with me the process of writing a book; to Jenny Emming, for your editing and encouraging words of wanting to gift a copy of my book to your beginning teacher niece; to Julie Purdy, my book designer, for working your magic and creating a pleasing product, of which I am proud. Thank you for so expertly and graciously guiding me on this exciting journey.

For You, My Readers

Please realize this book is in no way meant to be an arrogant appraisal of a life lived. It was written with the intent of sharing some of what I have learned with the hope that something may spark your imagination, be a springboard to a useful tool, or offer thoughts to consider as you plan for your days of teaching. In my fifty-five Septembers as both a student and teacher, I have learned much. I believe we are on this planet to help one another. If you find anything useful, then my purpose has been fulfilled.

Each vignette is titled to offer a quick summary as to its content. Some information is repeated, because my intention is for each vignette to stand alone and have meaning if it were the only selection read. Also, in order to protect the privacy of the individuals involved, no student names have been used and certain otherwise inconsequential details have been altered.

In the four sections, you'll find a mix: *My Mother's Vision* highlights my mother's resolve that I have an education, something she was denied beyond eighth grade; *My Early Years* focuses on remembered times that I consider pivotal to the woman I've become; *Things Learned While Teaching* offers useful strategies I have employed and perspectives that I believe made me a better teacher; *Odd and Ends* is just that, tossed in for good measure.

It is my hope that these entries will not disappoint. My intention is that they may offer five minutes of enjoyment or an afternoon's pleasure.

Table of Contents

Pictured with me is my family: son Allen, son John, and husband Tom, November 2012.

My Mother's Vision

*My parents, Irene and Mike Kosa, soon after
they were married, circa 1946.*

My Beginning

*A*fter his mother's death during the childbirth of his youngest sibling, my father was raised, in part, by his older sister and her husband. The farm they owned was located in a neighboring community of my mother's family's farm.

While in the Army fighting in Europe during World War II, my father was the only survivor when his tank was destroyed. He sustained severe burns, especially to his legs. The local paper ran an article about this event and gave his hospital address should anyone care to send him a card or to write him a note. My mother thought this to be a good idea and a nice thing to do, knowing of him but not actually knowing him. This correspondence blossomed into their marrying in October of 1946. A son was born two months prematurely in late 1947 and lived only a day. Three years later, I was born, also prematurely but only by one month. Seemingly, I didn't have a properly developed stomach lining and could keep nothing much down of needed nourishment. I appeared to be losing ground rapidly. My mother's doctor had already told her to be prepared to lose me, too.

As life would have it, an older German doctor was visiting the hospital, and his suggestion was to give me raw lemon juice, as he felt a little more acid with my food was just what I needed. For whatever reason, that proved to be true, and I survived, thrived even. As an aside, I still enjoy tart juices and fruit to this day.

Only Child of an Only Child

I am an only child of an only child on my mother's side, and that suits me just fine. I never longed for siblings, and I was perfectly happy living in an adult world, which truly is the only world I have ever known. We lived with my grandparents, as my grandmother had suffered a massive coronary prior to my birth, and back then, bed rest was required for about six months with full recovery being unsure. In those days, there was none of the "up the next day" for heart patients as we experience today.

By the time I was born, neither grandparent drove a car, so my mother was their chauffeur, furthering my contact with adults. I was literally taken on every trip, whether visiting neighbors and relatives or shopping. Usually there were no other children at the homes we visited as they were grown, so I sat and listened to the adults. This delighted me, and I soon identified the fascinating

*My mother, Irene, and I – a mother and
daughter so proud to be together.*

storytellers and those who couldn't hold a train of thought.
I would very quietly sit, endlessly listening. I loved it and feel I
gained a very real understanding of the adult world. To this day,
I interact very comfortably with the generation before mine. I
see them as people having the same wants, cares, hopes, and
dreams as my generation, just a bit more experienced.

Being an only child of an only child has afforded me the
opportunity to "pick" my family. I value that. Also, having had
two wonderful stepdads has made me realize as Richard Bach

has written in *Illusions*, "The bond that links your true family is not one of blood, but of respect and joy in each other's life. Rarely do members of one family grow up under the same roof."

Genealogy has never held a particular interest for me. I figure we are all part of the family of man.

My Mother's Vision

*M*y mother was an only child born in 1918 and was a teenager in the Great Depression. She loved school and longed for an education. My grandparents didn't think a girl needed any education beyond eighth grade and were not supportive of her attending high school. My mother walked the nearly four miles each way to attend ninth grade, but the bitter January winds won, and she dropped out of school.

Their attitude makes my grandparents seem very small and selfish to me, and they were people I loved so very much. But as a friend told me, "Mike, they thought they were doing the right thing by her. The times were different." Yes, they most certainly were.

My father left my mother for another woman when I was two years old, leaving her with me and nine dollars. In his defense, my father did pay child support, and I saw him every week of my life until he died the day after I turned thirty.

My mother's lack of an education, which she dearly desired, and being left with a two-year-old, nine dollars, and no job skills were the very reasons she wanted me to become educated. If she told me once, she told me a thousand times, "I want you to be able to stand on your own two feet." Thank you, Mother. I am typing this with the fingers of someone with a master's degree plus thirty-one credits. It's amazing what vision can do!

The Importance of My Education

*E*ven when I was a very little girl, I realized that my having an education was a top priority of my mother's. We went to my aunt's house near Clifford, and she gave me a dollar. Wow, was I happy! Remember this was probably 1953, and money was scarce. The very next day, with me in tow, my mother marched up the huge cement steps of the Akron State Bank. She had me by the hand as I couldn't quite reach the next step being so little. She boosted me with a tug as I climbed each step. Once inside, we went to a teller's window who was a family friend and neighbor. I can still close my eyes and see my mother's friend raising herself on her tiptoes and peering over the edge of the teller's window as she kindly asked me, "Michele, how may I help you?"

Even at that very young age, I knew the routine and the expected response. "I would like to put this in my college fund, please," I told her as I handed her the dollar bill.

"Why, of course," she replied with satisfaction, suggesting to me my mother was raising me right.

When we left, I knew my mother felt good and that a great plan was afoot. Truthfully, I would have rather spent the dollar on candy. Today, I marvel at my mother's optimism and vision with such a huge goal and meager beginnings.

The Mustard Seed Necklace

$\mathcal{I}$ distinctly remember a necklace that was given to my mother after my father left her for another woman. She was gifted it sometime during their divorce process. I recall the day that it was given to her by the local druggist (pharmacist today), who was a woman. While making our regular stop to procure my grandmother's medications, the necklace was on display in her store, which sold a variety of drugstore-type items. The druggist took the necklace from below the counter and gave it to my mother, telling her that she thought that she needed it.

It should be noted, considering her circumstances, that by any assessment my mother's future seemed bleak. The necklace was a gold chain with a spherical pendant that was clear except for the gold ring holding it and a mustard seed positioned in the center. Of course, the reference was to Jesus's words from *Matthew 17:15, "For truly, I say to you, if you have faith as a grain of mustard seed, you will say to this mountain, 'Move hence to yonder place,' and it will move; and nothing will be impossible to you."* My mother often wore that necklace, and I can vividly remember her grasping the pendant and saying with a far away look, "If ye but have faith."

She indeed had faith and nothing was impossible to her.

Hair-Washing Poetry

As long as I can remember, I have always loved poetry and words. My very favorite time of the week when I was a little girl was when my mother washed my long hair. While lying across the kitchen sink having my hair washed, she would recite poetry to me, and I loved it. I still enjoy poetry today. One of my very favorite poems was *In School Days* by John Greenleaf Whittier, which I can still recite.

Saving Coins

$\mathcal{T}$he coins: the quarters, dimes, nickels, and even pennies that my mother saved were gold to her, offering life improvements. Looking back, I realize that my mother had a very difficult financial existence. As a nursing assistant with no formal training, she earned one dollar an hour, forty dollars a week. This was in the early 1950s, so the money went farther than it does today, but that still wasn't much. Occasionally, she would receive a "bonus" five-dollar bill or, on more rare occasions, a ten. She took great pride in her ability to heal sores and care for patients. She truly loved her work and the patients.

My mother was always trying to better herself. I do remember her saving her change in a jar. The pennies, nickels, dimes, and quarters mounted as she tried to pay for everything in bills, saving the change. In this way, over a couple of years, my mother was able to afford some of the things that were considered luxuries at that time, at least by our family. One of her first purchases was a Smith-Corona, portable typewriter. Also purchasing a typing manual, she set her mind to learning to type correctly, no hunt and peck for her.

I remember her coming home from a day's work, eating supper, and sitting down at the desk in the corner of the living room with the lamp aglow, teaching herself to type. Of course, the manual had her practicing the qwerty keyboard. As I remember it now, she became quite skilled. Even at my young age, I was very, very proud of her accomplishments. In that time, there was no such thing as an electric typewriter. Sometimes it was a stiff tap, tap, tap for her. In later years, her arthritic fingers bothered her to the extent that holding a pen was easier but still somewhat cumbersome. But for many, many years, she typed letters and other documents on that faithful Smith-Corona.

Her goal was to better herself, and she found a way. She saved and scrimped until she could afford that typewriter, and then she taught herself to type. I think that says volumes about the kind of woman she was. She wanted something better, and she actively pursued it, overcoming great obstacles. She was an active participant in her life, aspiring and setting in motion things she wanted.

She was a wonderful role model for me.

The Freezer

$\mathcal{S}$aving coins made a big difference in my mother's life, affording her some of life's "luxuries." Saving coins from change over time is also how my mother was able to buy a freezer, the chest type. Our small Crosley refrigerator also had a small freezer section, but in truth, there wouldn't have been room for very much, let alone ice cream cartons. I doubt if the entire refrigerator were over a few cubic feet, including the freezer section, so not much could be kept frozen. As I remember, the freezer section was referred to as the icebox and had a couple of ice cube trays, the metal kind popular in that day, the kind with the insert that when you lifted the handle it loosened all of the cubes. All to say, there was no room for much of anything else. I remember my mother scrimping and saving for a freezer (or deep freeze as she called it) after earning her typewriter. It was an exciting day when I was able to go to the store with her while she selected the model. Even finer was the day that it was delivered to our home. We had a freezer!

In my view, the really big improvement the freezer meant to our lives was that we could buy ice cream! Almost nightly for over a year after its arrival, after eating supper (what dinner was called in our house) and finishing my homework or whatever chores we had, we would each have a bowl of ice cream. Each person (my grandparents, mother, and I) had a favorite kind, which was looked upon as an extravagance and luxury in itself. My grandfather's favorite was vanilla, something I still can't understand but realize it is the favorite of many today – my husband included. Grandma's favorite was butter pecan. My mother favored cherry nut with the big chunks of cherries, saying that she liked sinking her teeth into something. My favorite, you ask? Chocolate, of course; hey, I was a kid. To this day it is still my favorite, but I will take "things" tossed in today, like nuts, peanut butter, fudge chips, or whatever, to make it complete. The event of having a bowl of ice cream became a nightly ritual and usually occurred around eight o'clock in the evening, making a supreme memory for me.

I can still remember the coolness of the ice cream resting on my tongue, and the pride my mother felt of being able to have ice cream in our home. Before that time, it was a very extraordinary treat reserved only for special occasions and procured from the local ice cream fountain in town four miles from our home. On those newly found nights of luxury, I would even swallow small chunks of ice cream, so I could feel the clump make its way down my esophagus, relishing the whole experience. We had most definitely arrived.

I remember with great fondness how important being able to afford a freezer and ice cream whenever we wished were to my mother. I smile today as the Schwan's truck comes to our door bringing us ice cream galore and other food treats. It was such a special treat back then in the mid-1950s.

My folks, Bob and Irene Capling, with me in the center, at my retirement party in 2010.

My Mother Today

*Y*ou may wonder what has become of this dynamo of a mother with such a far-reaching vision for her daughter. Age has taken its toll, and as of this writing she is ninety-four. She and her husband, my second wonderful stepfather and one of forty years now, lived a couple of miles from me. I visited them daily. A few months ago, she fell down the stairs, and she is now residing in a local nursing home. Unfortunately, mother has dementia. Some days she knows me, and some days she's not quite as sure of whom I am. There are moments of clarity in which her humor and wit shine through untarnished by the disease and other times when she just doesn't know quite what to do. Her husband is amazing and still takes her for rides two or three times a week, weather permitting. About every couple of weeks, she will look at me and say, "You know (that is her phrase which means to listen well), I love you, and I love people." Yes, mother, I know, and so do I love you, and people, too.

*My
Early
Years*

This snapshot captured me showing off my cake on my fifth birthday in 1955.

My dog welcomed me home every day after school, 1958.

I'm all dressed up for my first day of fourth grade, 1959.

My Longest Friend

*A*s I have mentioned, I was born one month prematurely. This caused me to stay in the hospital for the first month of my life. While there, a woman (Thelma) came in and gave birth to a baby girl (Christena) nine days into my life. My mother met the woman while visiting me and soon learned that the woman and her family only lived four and a half miles southwest from where we lived. This was very close as we lived in farm country. They had not known each other previously, but became quick friends. Her baby girl stayed three or four days in the maternity ward, and I stayed another couple of weeks. I consider Chris's stay with me in the maternity ward to have been my very first slumber party.

During those few, brief days, this woman and my mother began a friendship that spanned their entire lifetimes. I could also rightly say that the baby girl became my very first friend and is still a dear friend of mine today.

While I was very little, my mother and father divorced. Dick and Thelma purchased a new car. Because their old car, a 1947 Chevy, was still in fine working condition and dependable, they sold it to my mother at the affordable price of $700. Many kindnesses were offered to my mother by Dick and Thelma throughout the years.

I distinctly remember going to Chris's fifth birthday party. One game seemed very hard to me, and I was shy being the only child of an only child and not having many playmates my own age. After taking off our shoes, we were to race across the room balancing a raw potato, one atop each foot, turn around, and return to the starting point. I could not imagine how this was going to work. Thelma spotted my reluctance and bent down to my level, flashed me her beautiful smile, and asked, "What's wrong?" I confessed that I didn't think I could do what was asked. She tossed her head back and laughed saying, "Oh, that's the fun of it, probably nobody can." That wonderful smile and pronouncement gave me permission to try. I had a terrific time at the party and now, some fifty-seven years later, remember Thelma's kindnesses to me.

Chris and I went to school together, riding the same school bus from kindergarten through fourth grade. Then, I moved ten miles south to another school district. Later, Chris's family built a new home, and she came to Caro for her senior year and to graduate.

Thelma and my mother remained friends over the years and would often ask Chris and me about each other. Both remarried (Thelma after Dick's death and my mom after my first stepdad's death) and kept in touch with each other. Another similarity was that both had dementia in their later years. Despite that, Chris told me that on the last trip with her mother from Saginaw to her assisted living apartment when traveling by Mother's crossroad, her mother said, "I wonder how Irene (my mother) is?" Chris told her that Irene was fine.

My longest friend, Chris (Campbell) Besonen, and I at my retirement party, July 2010.

Let it be also noted, that Chris became a school secretary and worked for the Caro Community School system for many, many years. After a while, she became the main secretary in our building, and we worked together for over twenty-five years prior to her retirement.

In recent years, I was also privileged to officiate Thelma's memorial service and the all too soon funeral of Chris's older son. Chris is indeed my longest friend.

The Sled

In 1961, my parents gave me a fiberglass, flying saucer sled for Christmas. That type of sled was somewhat new and novel. After opening gifts Christmas morning, Dad said that we would take it for a test run after finishing the chores.

Once all of the milking-related tasks were completed, he found a long rope, hooked it to the trailer hitch on our two-toned, green, 1956 Plymouth and told me to grab the other end. Off we went down the road heading north approaching speeds of 30 mph. Boy, was it fun! Our road was paved to Dixon Road, but not beyond the corner on which the Hile family lived. (Yes, that would be my now husband's family home.) Dad slowed for the corner and sped up once having crossed. The ride had been smooth and fun, but suddenly it was much less comfortable. My bottom was hurting big time. About half a mile down the road, I waved for my dad to stop. I stood up, picked up the saucer only to find holes ripped in it from the stones on the gravel road. Ouch! I had black-and-blue, rear-end bruises for a couple of weeks.

I accompanied him as he took it back to the hardware where it had been purchased. He told the owner and family friend that he wanted his money back, showing her the mutilated saucer.

She laughed and said, "What did you do, take it down a gravel road?" Yep, we did!

My Parents' View: Support the Teacher, Right or Wrong

*M*uch is written and said about parents. As far as I was concerned, parents made a great difference in a student's success or failure. In saying that, I must also say that I have seen many students rise above parents who didn't give a hoot about school and make their way in the world seeking a good education. Most times, given parents willing to work with me and support the school, wonderful things would happen. If the parent would back the school, magnificence was attainable. I held that as a possibility in every school in the nation, yes, every single one.

My dad would say to me, "A teacher may not always be right, but we're going to back the teacher 100 percent of the time, right or wrong. So, don't you ever come home whining and complaining about a teacher expecting us to back you. Yes, there may be times, as they are human, that the teachers might not be right, but we will still stand behind them and the school." In our house, it was that pure and simple for me. That

*My dad and mom, Harry and Irene Churchill, standing with
me celebrating graduation Sunday at our church after having
received my degree from Michigan State University in 1972.*

rule was hard and fast in my life, and I knew if I had trouble at
school that I would be in a lot bigger trouble at home.

My parents knew of a family with several children, and
it seemed like those kids always had bad teachers, at least
according to their parents. My dad said, "You know, I am sure
there are some teachers better than others; teachers may have
made a poor decision here or there, but I really can't believe
that every year their kids get seven bad teachers. If they would
support the school, what the school is trying to do with and for

their children, I think those parents would be a lot further ahead."
Well, as do I.

Have I always made the right decisions as a teacher? No, but when parents and I worked together presenting the united front that school mattered and that the child's education was important and that the student needed to do what I requested of him or her, absolutely amazing things happened.

Mr. Kreh

I still remember my first day of seventh-grade math class in the fall of 1962. Mr. Kreh (with whom I later taught for many years) "led" the class in a discussion of desirable characteristics of a class. He elicited from us those qualities, writing the words on the chalkboard, one underneath the other: Kindness, Recreation, Efficiency, and Honesty. We, all forty-three of us, were quite pleased with the list. He seemed especially so, too. Then he circled the first letters of the four traits we collectively deemed desired in a class, and they spelled his last name, Kreh. We, as seventh-graders, thought it a bit corny, yet kind of neat.

Kindness
Recreation
Efficiency
Honesty

It is odd what sticks with a person. I remember that so clearly as if it were yesterday, and it has been fifty years!

Seventh-Grade Me

I often told my middle school students that if they were anything like I was in seventh grade, I'd run out of the classroom screaming and never be back. It wasn't that I was wicked or malevolent, just annoyingly dippy. Realize there were forty-three of us in the "accelerated" section.

I wrote on the grout between the cement blocks to kids in other hours as we were shoved against the classroom walls.

In one hour, the girl in front of me had extremely long hair, and I would tie it to her chair. When the bell rang and she stood up, she would promptly be jerked back into her seat never ceasing to amuse me.

I was forever taking my foot and sliding the student's books out of his or her under-seat, desk rack in front of me.

In third hour with split lunch, another girl and I would exchange seats after lunch entirely certain that the teacher didn't know.

Back in that time, cartridge ink pens were the rage, and another student and I routinely had ink fights in math. He sat two seats to my left in the next to the last row of the classroom. A few days before Christmas vacation, the girl next to me wore a light ivory, taffeta dress with black velvet trim, very dressy and definitely not a school dress. While she was bending over getting her books, I slung ink at my friend. Wouldn't you know, she straightened herself in time to catch my ink with her ivory dress. I was sure I was dead meat. Interestingly, no repercussions resulted, but I never saw the dress again. However, that incident cured me of my ink fighting.

The kids I taught were tame compared to my annoying antics.

By eighth grade, I matured, became a well-behaved student, and never looked back.

Seating Charts

From junior high (That was what it was called in my day, not middle school.) through high school, most of my teachers sat their classes alphabetically using last names. This resulted in being in the same row or next to the same people day in and day out. Routinely, we had as many as forty-three in our section as I remember, so the classroom was full. For many of those classes, we sat Keinath, Kosa (me), and McComb with a random student occasionally interrupting the threesome, because there were others in our class with

Karen Keinath, Barb (McComb) Niesen, and I, pictured in 2011 and still dear friends, forty-nine years after being seated next to each other in the eighth grade.

names falling in that part of the alphabet but not normally in our particular section.

Karen Keinath had come into town school at the beginning of seventh grade as the country schools were being closed during that era. Barb McComb had come into town school a few years earlier when her rural school consolidated. Barb and Karen were first cousins with their mothers being sisters. My mother, being nine and eleven years older than their mothers, respectively, babysat their mothers years earlier as they grew up across the section from one another.

Keinath, Kosa, and McComb became fast friends and remain so today fifty years later. We now gather for dinner one night a month. Barb and I roomed together for our first three years of college at Michigan State before she married. Karen and I were in her wedding. Both were in my wedding three years later.

When I returned to teach in my hometown, Barb's father was president of the board of education that hired me.

In recent years, I officiated the wedding of Barb's youngest child. Of course, Karen was there, and we sat together at the reception.

We three have remained dear friends over these many, many years. I have often wondered how those methodically made seating charts set the course of our lives and friendships. In the fifty years since first being seated in that alphabetical order, we are friends caring for one another still.

Gladys Wiltse: My First Life Mentor

*P*robably because of writing of my earlier school days, I have been thinking about Gladys Wiltse's influence on my life. My parents were terrific, but I do feel outside influences are often apt to be the ones to which we tie our dreams. Our parents are such known entities that often their influences seem innate. Of course, now at my age, I do realize the wonderful impact and influence my life has been given by my folks, but that initial, teen influence was Gladys Wiltse, or the Great Gladys Wiltse as I like to think of her.

I was privileged to deliver Gladys Wiltse's eulogy, being asked by her children at the visitation if I would like to say a few things about their mother at her funeral the following day. I was honored to do so.

I thought you might like to read the thoughts of a former student about her ninth-grade teacher. Gladys was ninety-four when she passed, and I was fifty-two.

If you have been a teacher, know there are students you have taught who feel about you as I felt about Gladys.

My life mentor, Gladys Garner Wiltse, the woman who showed me I could be the person I am today.

IN MEMORY OF GLADYS GARNER WILTSE
February 27, 2003
by Michele Kosa Hile

In the fall of 1964, nearly forty years ago, I walked into Gladys Wiltse's ninth-grade civics and Michigan history class, and my life was changed forever. Please understand, I had great parents and I don't want to take anything away from them, but the wisdom of one's parents is often lost on fourteen-year-olds. I was a ditzy, fourteen-year-old girl with issues, and I soon came to realize the influence Gladys Wiltse had on me. Besides my parents, she was the most influential person in my life, shaping the person I have become today, followed by Suzanne Harwick, also a former member of this church (First Presbyterian Church of Caro, Michigan).

When you walked into Gladys Wiltse's classroom, you knew the playing field was level and that you would be treated with dignity and respect, as a person of worth. Gladys would enable, encourage, and inspire us to be the very best we could be. She set the bar high, but it was always within reach. She saw the worth of the individual. Gladys believed we could make a difference in the people we were to become by making positive choices. She believed we held the keys to our futures in our hands, reflected in the choices we made. Our lives were in our control.

I can close my eyes and still see her at various places in her classroom teaching us. I can recount at least a dozen of the stylish outfits she wore, remember where she was standing in the room, and see her gesturing and hear her voice. She taught us about life and shared her love for Michigan history.

Gladys Wiltse was also the Michigan History Club Advisor. I was a member and an officer all four years of high school. Her enthusiasm for Michigan history was evident. She would take us to Hickory Island Cemetery on M-25 or to the Juniata Township (Watrousville) Cemetery in search of the graves of Civil War veterans, an extensive county-wide project she engineered. We also did documentation work at the petroglyphs just east of Cass City and presented our findings to the Michigan Historical Society's annual meeting. Each year, she would take the entire history club (as many as sixty students) to Mackinac Island for a two- or three-night stay. Just imagine that! (Kay Montei and I are the Academic Track coordinators, and we take the team all over the Thumb and the Saginaw area. When I am riding the bus with the kids, I think of the hundreds of miles that I traveled with Gladys on one school trip or another.)

After high school, I attended Michigan State University and became a teacher, returning to Caro in the fall of 1972. My first year teaching was Gladys's last. She was my mentor. At the end of many long, hard, exhausting days, I would make my way up the hall to Gladys's room. She would encourage and uplift me, sharing teaching techniques she employed to successfully teach. We shared some of the same students and would reflect on their off-the-wall behavior on certain days. She was always there for me. In addition to being a colleague, we became friends, dear friends. At the end of my first year teaching, I traveled completely around the world with Gladys and her husband as their granddaughter's roommate. Then, we spent part of the following summer in the British Isles traveling together.

I wasn't going to mention this, but I chuckled when I read the quote from her niece, Suzanne, in today's program, "Holding back the best isn't the way Aunt Gladys lives her life." How true!

Three years ago, I had breast cancer. Some of my friends felt this was a wake-up call from the Universe for me to slow down, relax, and not be involved in so many community activities. I, however, took it to mean just the opposite. Life is very precious, and I need to maximize each moment. So, I move on with more intensity, effort, and gusto than ever before. I learned this lesson, in part, from Gladys.

I have spent many an hour sitting at her kitchen table, by the bowed window, talking or curled up on the north end of the couch while she sat in her chair. We would talk about life, what was important to each of us, or just visit. Those hours are precious to me.

If I had to describe Gladys Wiltse in one word, that word would have to be integrity. At our house, when you take the dictionary off the shelf, flip through the pages, come to the "I's" and continue until you find the word integrity, Gladys Wiltse's picture is right beside the entry. It's that pure and simple for me. Gladys Wiltse had more integrity than any person I have ever known.

I'm sure you know, Shari and Norm, that I loved your mother dearly. She most certainly brought out the very best in me. Besides my parents, she has had more influence on my life than any other person. She immeasurably has influenced the person I have become, and the teacher, and the community member. It has been said, "Duty is a matter of the mind. Commitment is a matter of the heart." Gladys Wiltse was committed. She loved this community. She taught ninth grade; I teach eighth grade. I am now in my thirty-first year teaching eighth grade at Caro Middle School just a few blocks down the street. I plan to teach at least nine more years before I contemplate retirement. I serve the community on five boards: three as secretary, one as treasurer, and chair two committees on the other. I don't tell you these things to highlight my life. I tell you these things so that you will know that the torch has been passed. The lessons Gladys Wiltse taught were not lost on me. I endeavor to walk in her footsteps. She believed if you wanted a better community then you had a responsibility in making it so. I believe that also, a lesson learned at her side.

In my classroom, I have had up on the wall for the last several years (new renditions, of course) the words *I teach because...* followed by six different endings to that sentence starter. *I teach because... ...I like school; ...it's fun; ...I enjoy learning; ...I want the best possible life for you.* Now, I am telling you this for these last two endings. *I teach because ...my teachers believed in me; ...I believe in you.* Gladys Wiltse believed in me. Every time I look up in my classroom and read that fifth line, *...my teachers believed in me*, I think of Gladys Wiltse and Suzanne Harwick. Every time. They are with me daily in my classroom as I teach my students, reminding me of the teacher and person I should be. Gladys Wiltse saw beyond the ditzy, fourteen-year-old girl with issues to the woman I was capable of becoming. I am still striving to be that person every day, some nearly forty years later. Yes, Gladys Wiltse believed in me, and for that I shall be eternally grateful.

*Suzanne Harwick, my second life mentor, who ignited
my lifelong excitement for biology and who inspired
me to be the best teacher I could be.*

Tenth-Grade Biology

*A*fter leaving ninth grade, I knew that I wanted to be a teacher but was unsure as to the grade level and subject. In the fall of 1965, I had Suzanne Harwick for tenth-grade biology. We were her only section of biology with the rest of her day spent teaching seventh-grade reading and spelling. Happily being a farm girl, I had always enjoyed science. She arranged for us to dissect seven animal organisms that year. I was mesmerized by the intricate detail exhibited within the animals' bodies and knew I had found my calling.

When I was a senior in high school, I was a cadet teacher for Suzanne in one of her seventh-grade reading and spelling classes. I learned much from those days as I corrected papers, organized materials, tutored students, presented lesson snippets under her watchful eye, and did a variety of errands. For me, she was a master teacher setting the standard of a well-run classroom, and I learned much.

In later years when I began teaching, we taught in the same hall. Upon her retirement, I took over her seventh-grade reading and spelling classes for a few years, having a master's in secondary reading instruction, before returning to teaching science.

I owe her a great deal for the teacher and woman I have become. We became and remain lifelong friends.

The Day I Decided to Go to Michigan State

Summer school was offered after my tenth-grade year. In addition to remedial classes, an advanced writing class was scheduled and was taught by my tenth-grade English teacher, whom I dearly enjoyed. We had always gotten along well, and

I had especially appreciated her precision in teaching grammar. I believed an advanced writing class would better prepare me for college. She had, assisting with that class, a girl from our town who was, at that time, a junior in college. She was going to be a teacher, and this class was the perfect opportunity for her to earn money and hone her craft while being home for the summer.

One day at the end of a break, the assistant asked each of us where we thought we'd like to go to college. I said, "Well, I would like to go to Michigan State, but it's just too big." At that time there were more students attending Michigan State University daily than lived in our entire rural county: 45,000 students.

She replied, "I'll tell you something. I go to Albion, and it's a small college with about 3,000 students. But I know about twenty to twenty-five students well. The rest, I really don't know. Oh, I could recognize many of them, but I don't know them." She continued to tell me that wherever I would go, I would become good friends with about twenty to twenty-five others, and the size of the school really didn't matter as that number would basically stay the same. I would have that nucleus of friends, whether at a huge university or a small college; the approximate saturation of good friends' quota, so to speak, would be similar. With all the rest, many or few, you would simply not have particularly close connections. She strongly suggested that I not let the size of the school be the determining factor for not attending if there were other aspects I liked. In my view, there were many other advantages to Michigan State with the overall size of the student population being the only stumbling point.

That afternoon, I hopped on the tractor and cultivated navy beans until evening. Her insight led me to make up my mind that day to go to Michigan State, and I never looked back.

Here I am, after a day happily driving tractor, working on the family farm.

Several years later, I was invited to her nephew's graduation open house as I had been his eighth-grade science teacher. She was there, and I was finally able to tell her that the words she said that one summer day long ago allowed me to give myself permission to attend Michigan State University. Interestingly, at the time of our talking, her husband was a professor there.

I know many think Michigan State is huge, and it is. But if you're used to farm country, it's like the back forty. I have been ever grateful for her advice and wisdom. Interestingly, I now have two degrees from MSU as do my husband and our two sons. GO SPARTANS; GO GREEN!

The Power of a Compliment

$\mathscr{M}$y huge life mentor and ninth-grade civics teacher Gladys Wiltse enjoyed antiques. I had a great-aunt and uncle who had no children. Since we lived close to them my first ten years of life, my mother was like a daughter to them. In fact, my aunt lived in our home after my uncle needed convalescent care from the fall of my being in seventh grade through my junior year in high school. After their deaths, my mother had the task of clearing their home of its contents. As they had many well preserved antiques, we asked Mrs. Wiltse if she would like to look at them before we passed them on to others. In August after my junior year, Mrs. Wiltse came to our home, and we went to my aunt and uncle's home to view their antiques.

Over the years, I have enjoyed caring for our lawn (and still do) and always have been particular, fussy even, with the trimming, believing that simple act marks a well groomed yard setting it apart from an average lawn mowing job. Early in the week, Mrs. Wiltse came to our home before our driving her the eleven miles to our aunt and uncle's home. I had mowed the lawn the previous weekend.

I remember as she got out of her car, we exchanged hellos, and I invited her to come into our house for a moment while we finished getting ready to go. As she climbed the steps of our porch, she paused and looked out at our yard and said, "My, it certainly is neat here. You have a lovely yard."

I can assure you that I have had a lovely yard ever since that day with respect to the lawn's care and grooming as much as possible.

Some people don't see trimming as important in lawn care, but it is my forté. People will often comment that our lawn looks particularly nice. They don't realize trimming is that little extra "umph" that sets the yard apart making it look complete. I enjoy giving our lawn that finishing touch trimming with my line trimmer, so much so that I have regularly trimmed a friend's lawn for nearly twenty years.

All to say, it is now over forty-five years after Mrs. Wiltse's compliment, and I am trimming my lawn with that extra "umph" and telling you, my readers, about a compliment I received from one of my beloved teachers on a summer's day long ago. You have no idea the life of a compliment sincerely given. Give many to your students. There are those who will remember and cherish them forever.

Dad

Having recounted Gladys Wiltse's influence on the woman I became, I would be remiss not to mention my first stepdad, the person I think of as my dad even though I saw my biological father every week of my life until his death in 1980, the day after my thirtieth birthday. Mom married my stepdad July 30, 1960, and we moved to the home in which I am still living. He was fun and very community-minded, being active in many organizations. His vision for my life was wonderful, absolutely wonderful. He was in my life as my stepfather for only twelve years and four days, until his sudden death in 1972. Those twelve years, seemingly so short now, were the significant, formative years from ten until twenty-two.

Dad had been a bachelor in the community, providing horses for the area kids to use in 4-H. As a 4-H leader, he took club members to Michigan State University, the nation's premier land grant university, for various programs. He was a huge fan of the university. He expected me to attend college somewhere, and I knew he would be happy for it to be MSU. I also wanted to go to MSU once deciding it was not too big, the subject of an earlier vignette.

My great-aunt, who lived with us for five years while I was in seventh through eleventh grades after her husband had a stroke, left my mother some money for my education when she died in 1967. She had always said, "I want someone in the family to know something," referring to me. By the time I was a senior in high school, my parents had a prosperous dairy farm, and my dad was determined to pay for every cent of my college education. This he did, saving my aunt's money, which my mother later used after his death.

Graduation day from college was a very proud day. I was the first one of my family to be a college graduate. My college roommate, her family, and my family had a little celebration in our apartment after the commencement exercises. Looking back on that day, the handwriting was probably on the wall that my dad didn't have too long to live. For a few years, he had held the belief that he had cancer. His mother had died from cancer when she was in her thirties or early forties, and his brother had died in his fifties from cancer just a year or so before my graduation. My dad was fifty-seven. As a little boy, he had polio, leaving him with curvature of the spine and a hunched back. As he aged, his rib cage was settling, putting pressure on his internal organs. He had been hospitalized that June and thoroughly checked for cancer, of which they found none.

I had planted all of the navy beans as he was recovering. That was something easily done by me, as I was his right-hand man on the farm for many years. Dad wasn't up to walking to Spartan Stadium from the spot we would have to park. My Aunt Marion and Uncle Tim came and went to the ceremony with my mother. It was a gloriously happy day. Dad stayed in our apartment, slept, and rested. Celebrating that day, as I look back now, must have been a day filled with triumph for him. His vision of my going to Michigan State University and receiving a degree had been accomplished.

After graduation from college as a certified teacher and the teaching jobs being few, my dad was certain that our local superintendent would hire me. I was not particularly interested in teaching in Caro and had always thought that I would go to college, meet someone, marry, and live in a suburb of Chicago or some other large city. Not that I thought there was anything wrong with coming home to teach, as some others had done before me for various reasons. Some returned to marry spouses established in the area or had other business interests. I just thought, for me, that wasn't an option.

I was always the outdoors type, taking care of the lawn from a very young age. I did wonder who would mow the lawn when I lived in that big city suburb knowing my parents were too frugal to actually hire a lawn care service. I did express this concern to them. One spring when my parents picked me up from college for the weekend, my dad told me that he had mowed the lawn. I thought this was progress and couldn't wait to see what kind of a job he had done, as I was always very fussy having the lawn immaculate. As we drove in the yard, I noticed rather long grass, maybe a foot high, with a perfect figure eight cut in the back lawn. That was my dad's idea of a joke, but it left me wondering still, "What will happen to our lawn when I move to a career in some far-away city?"

Teaching jobs were very tight in 1972. There had been a teacher shortage a few years earlier, and so many of us had taken the challenge to become teachers that there was an over abundance. I interviewed with my home school at my dad's urging. The junior high principal interviewing me had been my seventh-grade reading and spelling teacher. I was his student during his first year of teaching. During the interview, he pulled open a drawer and said, "Here are fifteen hundred (yes, 1,500) applications. Why should we hire you?" Please understand, I believe he said so kindly but with definite interest in my answer. I have no idea what I mumbled, but it must have been sufficient.

The Wednesday following that interview, I received the call after lunch time. We always stopped our farm work to eat lunch, so my dad and I were in from the fields. My dad routinely had a nap after lunch before returning to the farm work. For many years, my mother took in and redistributed things people didn't want: the end of garage sales, a few sacks of things no longer useful, recycled linen, or whatever. I remember that day a pogo stick had come our way. While my dad napped, I tried my skill at pogo-sticking. When my mother told me that I had a phone call, I was huffing and puffing. There was no caller ID in those days. I received "the call" from the superintendent who my dad was so sure would hire me, asking me if I would like to be a teacher for Caro Community Schools. "Yes, I do. Wow, I'll take it!" I was thrilled; my dad was thrilled.

One week and one day after that fateful call on a Thursday, my dad had a debilitating stroke in the morning and died the following night. His job was done. His mission was accomplished. I was not only a Michigan State University graduate and teacher, I was a teacher for Caro Community Schools, my home-town school.

Mom and Dad (Irene and Harry Churchill, my first stepfather) on their wedding day, July 30,1960.

Milking in the Ice Storm

*W*hen my mom married my dad (first stepfather, actually), I was ten. They very soon bought a dairy herd. He was already a farmer, as was my mother's background growing up with her parents on their family farm. The dairy herd would provide a regular income, a stable base. A neighbor not too far away was selling his dairy herd as he was retiring. We picked up five or so cows from him and then one or two here and there from other local farmers. Soon a herd of nine to twelve was housed in our cow barn. We always had Holsteins with one Guernsey or Jersey to boost the butterfat content of the milk. My mother loved the cattle and had an excellent eye for them. It was well known that we had the cleanest barn on the milk route, and you could probably eat in the milk house with it being as sanitary as anyone's kitchen. In fact, my mother even routinely brushed the cattle and bleached the tails of those who were white. Our barns were spotless.

I was afraid of anything with four feet larger than a kitten, but fortunately we had very tame and friendly cattle. I was neither a horseman nor a cattleman. However, I really did like them. The trouble I saw with animals, including my favorite horse that would faithfully wait for me when I fell off, was that they required being fed and cared for every day. Conversely, the machinery, the tractors, and such could be parked and returned to days or a few weeks later and all was fine. Check the oil and put fuel in the tractors, and they were ready to go. No daily maintenance was required. But those cattle took daily time and care, lots of it.

Although I was not particularly good with the cattle, when my dad was scheduled to be hospitalized one winter for minor surgery, I came home to milk for a week. The surgery was scheduled during my Christmas break from college, perfect timing. While my dad was still in the hospital, as luck would have it, an ice storm occurred, leaving our area without power. Inspired by I am not quite sure what, I had the thought, "Mary's (our token Jersey to boost our milk's butterfat content) gentle; I'll try milking her by hand." Now realize that was something that

I had never done with the exception of a few brief squirts to an awaiting cat. After my relatively unsuccessful efforts of twenty minutes, Mary looked back at me and laid down ending my first and only milking by hand session. Thankfully, about an hour later the power was restored, and I successfully finished using the milking machines.

I am certainly not disparaging of the cattle as they paid for my college education, every cent of it. When I graduated from college in June of 1972, my parents sold the cattle as their mission was accomplished. The barn with a dozen head of milking cows served its purpose well. Although I wasn't particularly good with the cattle, I owed them a great debt. Because of them, I was launched, armed with the college education my mother was determined that I have.

Multitasking

*A*s a teacher, I was a master of multitasking. In addition to delivering my curriculum, I was constantly assessing classroom behavior, mood, and understanding and shifting my emphasis whenever required. My classroom management was akin to a master juggler's act. The more I could multitask and monitor and assess the classroom climate, the more effective my teaching was.

While on the topic of multitasking, I believe if anyone is to ever achieve successfully being two places at once, I will be one of the first, having many interests and liking to do many things.

Here is a true story to illustrate my point. When I attended Michigan State University, the school year was divided into terms, only switching to semesters in 1989 or so long after I had graduated. A term typically lasted ten weeks, and a normal year was three terms: fall, winter, and spring.

Going into spring term freshman year, I needed organic chemistry and trigonometry. My schedule was such that I had to go into "the pit" at the Men's IM. The pit was huge, the frustrations many, and the outcome unsure. MSU was in the early phase of computer scheduling as you had to pick up a computer card for a class, put your name and student number on it, and return it "to be run" at a later time. As I said, I needed two classes: organic chem and trig. Both classes had one section open; however, both were for the same time slot, 9:10 a.m., Monday through Friday. What to do? Notices were posted and supervisors stated, "The computer will not allow a student to register for two classes at the same time." Hmmm, I wondered. If the computer wouldn't allow me to register for two classes at the same time, I decided to do just that and take the class that I was given assuming one would be ejected. At least, I would have one and not run the risk of being "bumped" (due to over enrollment) from both. I thought it an excellent plan and executed it. My worries were over; whichever class I was given would be the one I would take, picking up the other at a later date.

A few days later, when our schedules were delivered to the dorm mailboxes, much to my surprise, I was scheduled for both classes. Yes, I had been scheduled for two different classes at exactly the same time! It seemed the computer did, in fact, let me do that very thing the signs said it wouldn't! Now, the prudent, thinking student would have contacted the registrar's office and dropped one class. Organic chem was four credits with a lab, which met once weekly for a two-hour block at another time so the lab was very doable. Trig was a lecture session five days a week with two afternoon recitation meetings, which I could also invariably attend. Attribute it to spring being in the air, but for whatever reason, I decided to keep the schedule and take both classes meeting exactly the same time determining that I could live through ten weeks of anything. Today, I would be concerned, if accomplished, that I wouldn't be granted credit, for it is still normally deemed impossible to be in two places at once. That was not a concern of mine back in the spring of 1969.

I went to trig on Mondays, Wednesdays, and Fridays and tried to make all of the recitation sessions whenever possible. I attended organic chem on Tuesdays and Thursdays and *never* missed the Friday lab, which thankfully met at a different time. I am sure you are wondering how all of this worked and if I received credit for anything.

By the third week of trig, I was becoming somewhat lost. By week six, I was pretty much hopelessly lost, but did not drop the class. By week seven, I stopped going to the regular class and attended one or both of the recitations, copying a few sample problems attempting to understand them. I also stayed "under the radar" and never volunteered to answer problems or anything else in class. I bravely went to the final exam carrying a 1.0 average, a 1.5 was passing. The class was five credits.

At this point, you must understand that my parents both had an eighth-grade education and highly valued education and deeply wanted better for me than they had, much better. They also trusted me, their bright daughter, to ably be in charge of her education. They worked their fingers to the bone, making sure an excellent education was mine, paying every cent. My dad often said that going to school and becoming educated was my job. They would not have been pleased (money-wise and time-wise) if I did not earn credit for a class. They had no idea that I was taking two classes at once.

I went to the trig exam and did the best I could, but in truth, I recognized very little but persisted in trying all of the problems. Much to my relief and amazement when I went to the mailbox that summer's day and received my grades; I had earned a 1.5 in trig. (They were actually sent to my parents, but they felt they were mine as an only child is afforded adulthood status early.) It was enough to pass; five credits earned. It must be noted that this was the last math class required for my major. Don't ask me any trig today, please.

Now to organic chemistry, four credits were at stake/risk. On the very first day of class, all three hundred of us were told by our professor that the curve would be such that half of the class would fail. I realize now what an enormous money maker that policy was for the university! But we were the baby boomers, and our parents wanted the best for us and expected us to want the same and earn it, too. No questions asked. That was an ominous prospect alone, but my situation compounded the threat having two classes at the same time. I religiously and faithfully attended the organic chem lab section every week. I had a good lab partner, and we made sure we knew what the purpose was for the class and executed the directions precisely. I knew for my lab portion that I had a 4.0 going into the exam, but that was a small component of the final grade. I found the basic subject engaging, especially the interesting asides like how Ivory Soap was a huge mistake with too much air being infused into the mix. Rather than toss the enormous batch, the company decided to market it as an advantage: Ivory, the soap that floats. It caught on and became its signature for many years added to the fact that it was lacking many of the oils and perfumes of other soaps. While wearing contacts for 37 years, I used Ivory soap daily because of its purity.

Back to the story, going into the exam I had a 0.5, yes, zero point five – not even close to passing. Organic chem was my last exam on Thursday night at 8:00 p.m. at 109B Anthony Hall on Shaw Lane. My other exams were completed Tuesday morning. I spent from Tuesday morning until exam time with the book (fairly small and blue) memorizing formulas. I was a decent memorizer, still am. I ate, slept little, and memorized lots and lots! I went to the exam with the thought that I had nothing to lose (carrying a 0.5) but only something to gain. Interestingly, after the exam I walked to the bus stop where other exam takers were gathered as we waited for buses to take us to our various destinations. The talk was about how hard the exam was, not encouraging but perplexing. I had thought I actually knew quite a bit of it and felt marginally optimistic. It had not completely baffled me. Their conversations made me a bit more concerned as they were classmates who had gone to each and every class. I adopted the attitude that it was done, and I did what I could.

Now waiting for grades with a possible failure in nine credits was not fun. But it was summer, I was home in the tractor seat I loved, and I would deal with the consequences when the time came if necessary. I full well knew that my parents would see it as a mistake in judgment and pay for me to retake the classes with the expectation of my passing both the next time. They had complete faith in me and my abilities, recognizing I was human. Of all the parents I knew, mine would have taken the news of failure best. If the truth were to be known, they would have never had to have known, as I was in charge of my education and they would without questions write the checks. My guilt, however, would have been much harder to assuage. The time passed; the mail with the registrar's grade report came. My final organic chem grade was a 2.0, respectable even. I had improved from a pre-exam score of 0.5 to a 2.0. I had aced the exam! I still know some organic chem today and can definitely follow articles written on the subject.

All to say, I earned nine credits back in the spring of 1969 with the classes being held simultaneously, which was multitasking to the max. HOORAY!

For the record, whenever I tell this story (I was the featured alumni speaker at the high school academic letters ceremony in 1997.), I do forewarn others not to do as I did.

Being Interviewed in Ohio

*U*pon earning my bachelor's degree and being awarded a provisional teaching certificate from the state of Michigan, I set upon finding a job. My dad always felt that the superintendent of my home school would hire me, but I was looking to greener pastures. I sent applications to Chicago suburbs and several other places, but it was 1972 and teachers were in surplus virtually everywhere.

I landed an interview in Lancaster, Ohio, and drove there to be shown the facilities. Another prospective teacher had also been summoned for the day. We were the finalists: one position, two people. The town seemed pleasant and the people friendly. The other candidate and I were taken on a tour, fed, and questioned in general. Nearing the end of the day, we were then interviewed separately by the superintendent. I was first.

The interview seemed to be going well, and I ventured to ask the salary. The superintendent very proudly stated, "$5,900," to which I replied, "$5,900!" Ohio did not require a college major and a minor as Michigan did, making Michigan graduates particularly desirable. Ohio was less stringent in its overall requirements and its pay, respectively. I was in shock as the closest in salary of the other jobs for which I had applied was my home town's $8,320. I was an only child of an only child (still am), and did not plan to have a roommate. It was unimaginable living alone in another state and making ends meet on $5,900, even if it were 1972. I have no idea how the interview ended but the figure $5,900 kept reverberating in my head. I was stunned and numb. The other candidate was sitting in the outer office, and I was told to tell her to go in to see the superintendent upon my leaving. I am hoping I left gracefully, but I still am not too sure of that.

I staggered out of the office and walked over to her. I asked her if she knew this job paid only $5,900, feeling I had completely wasted my time and money on the trip. She smiled brightly and said, "Oh yes, it is one of the highest paying schools in Ohio!" I assume she was offered the job.

Being Hired at My Home School

*B*eing hired at my home school to teach junior high was a disappointment. Of course, I was certainly thankful to be employed as teaching jobs were very scarce in 1972. Of the dozen or so other education majors with whom I had been friendly in college, there were only two of us who were hired as full-time teachers that first fall. Many spent their lives in different careers or were hired after doing some other jobs for a long while, years in some cases. At the time of my hiring, I was looking to the big city, possibly Chicago, and a job away from home, and most certainly not junior high school. When I began, I expected to stay two years at the very longest.

Back in those early days, it was customary for the junior high teachers to teach a high school class at the end of the day. I did that for six years. In the beginning, those classes were large, and I remember one in which 57 percent (I did the math.) was taking the class for the second time having failed it the first. Over time, when the students could pick me having known me from junior high, I had excellent classes. But I will tell you that the high school students just sat there and looked at me for the most part with a "teach me" attitude. They were very sedate and seemingly above becoming too involved. On the other hand, the junior high kids were all over the place. They had energy; all I had to do was channel it. They were very easily led, and they were tons of fun. I quickly found, they were "my people." Junior high students rarely sat back but were instead trying to all talk at once, telling you this or that, related to class or otherwise. They were never quiet or dull or laid back, but always wonderfully fun and engaging. Over the years, I have decided that I have the personality of an eighth-grader; no wonder we always got along so well.

By the time I retired, I had been the most seniored science person in our school system for several years. You couldn't pry me out of junior high, which over the years, became termed middle school. There would have been deep heel marks in the tile if I had been forced to go to the high school. I think being "misplaced" in junior high was one of the greatest blessings of my life.

An unexpected benefit of returning home to teach was that a half mile down the road lived a man whom I had always known and enjoyed, who would become my husband. Tom was seven years older than I and still is. He would buy seed corn from my dad, and I always liked visiting with him. From Caro High School, he had gone to the Massachusetts Institute of Technology before returning to Michigan and earning his bachelor and master's degrees from Michigan State University. I always found him very interesting and thought he had wonderful things to say. Being hired in my home school and living in the house I grew up in (my mother left to marry my second stepfather shortly after the death of my dad) gave me the opportunity to marry this wonderful man, the father of our two sons. The former appeal of a big city was soon forgotten. In returning to teach in my home school, I found my life.

Dad's Funeral Home Visitation

*T*wo things in particular stand out in my memory about the visitation period at the funeral home for my dad. First, Dick Harwick, my high school biology teacher's husband, told me that he had seen my dad on the street one day. He mentioned what a nice girl his wife thought that I was, to which my dad responded, "We intend she be." Dick's comment detailed how matter-of-fact my dad had been as if that, indeed, were the plan.

The second encounter was with a long-time farmer, bachelor friend of my dad's. My dad had been a bachelor until he married my mother at the age of forty-five. His friend just stood in the doorway before getting to the guest book. From there, he looked at me and said, "Well, you lost your buddy." Yes, I lost my buddy. I was Dad's shadow on the farm and in life for many years.

My Job Opportunity

$\mathscr{T}$eaching positions were tight in the summer of 1972. I found work at my home school, and I am still not too sure as to why I, in particular, was hired. Maybe, the administration wanted to help its former graduates succeed. I really don't know, as I am very sure there were many qualified people with credentials equally as fine as mine.

Anyway, a junior high science teacher was pregnant with her third child and was taking a few years off to be at home with her growing family. She and her husband had begun teaching in Caro when I was in eighth grade in the fall of 1963. It was nine years later when I was job hunting. I had the husband for eighth-grade math with forty-two other students. I did not have his wife but knew her to be very popular and a wonderful teacher, as was her husband.

For whatever reason, I was awarded the job. Her baby girl was born in Caro Community Hospital adjacent to our school on September 7, I believe a Thursday, 1972. During our lunch hour, three of us ventured over and stood outside the hospital room's window on a soggy lawn from a recent rain and viewed the beautiful, newborn, baby girl. We could not actually go in the hospital and see the baby as the thought of the day was that we would contaminate her and ruin her for life.

That baby girl grew, became a well respected teacher, and I taught with her for over fifteen years before retiring.

Rewarding Myself

*D*uring the summer after my first year of teaching, I was fortunate to have the opportunity to travel completely around the world. Originally, I had planned to go to visit my student teaching supervisor and his family in Japan. He and his wife had taught in Japan at an American school before returning to the States and having their two children. That summer, they were returning to Japan planning to stay a couple of months, and invited me to join them for two or three weeks.

As it happened, I was living alone in the house on the family farm where I grew up (and my husband and I still live), which meant that I did not have to pay rent. The savings on housing could be spent on travel.

My life's mentor, Gladys Wiltse, her husband, and their fifteen-year-old granddaughter were scheduled to travel around the world that summer on an organized trip with a travel group. The plan was to go with the Wiltses as far as Japan and then stay a few weeks with my student teaching supervisor's family before returning home with them later in the summer.

About three weeks before leaving, I received word that my supervisor's family would be taking a steamer and traveling to India just a bit after I would be arriving in Japan to visit them. I was welcome to travel with them and sincerely invited. This would mean cramped accommodations with a family of four with two of the four being children under five. I declined and decided to stay with the around the world trip making it a twenty-six-day vacation. I viewed the trip as my reward for surviving my first year of teaching.

We left June 23, 1973, from Tri-City Airport, as it was then called, MBS today. We flew to Detroit and then on to JFK in New York. Drinks were served at 10:00 a.m. in flight to Detroit. I still have no idea what possessed me, but I had a Scotch and water on a relatively empty stomach making it a very long day. My head was spinning in Detroit as I sat slumped in a chair awaiting our flight to New York. By the time we arrived in New York, I had rallied and was feeling fine. From New York, it was a seven-hour flight in a Boeing 707 to Athens, Greece. From Greece, we traveled to Egypt, Lebanon, India, Iran, Thailand, fueled in South Vietnam, Hong Kong, Taipei, Japan, Alaska, Seattle, Chicago, and home. Once leaving Alaska, we were in transit for the other stops and only saw the airports. As we were returning home, flying over Tri-City in mid-July with the golden wheat fields and vibrant bean and corn fields, an appreciation of home overwhelmed me.

The trip was wonderful, and we stayed at first class hotels. Our hotel in Egypt was the same one that President Nixon and Secretary of State Henry Kissinger had stayed just a few weeks before we did. My reward for surviving my first year of teaching was the trip of a lifetime!

Things Learned While Teaching

Back in the Day

*F*or my first six years of teaching, I had a high school class at the end of the day. That was a common practice back then. In January of 1976, I was told that the administration was unsure as to just what my last hour class would be. My undergraduate major was biology with a physical science minor, and I had taken plenty of math classes. I was assigned students, and they came the first day still not knowing just what the class would be. I improvised doing a current events type of class, relating the topics to science and applying math.

On the second day of class, after much pressure from me as to what I was to be teaching, an administrator overseeing curriculum came into my classroom. He asked the students how many needed a science credit. Several raised their hands. Next, he inquired as to how many needed a math credit. More signaled this need. He turned to me in front of the entire class and announced, "Mrs. Hile, this will be a math class."

As he left, I followed him to the hallway and inquired as to books and exactly what type of a math class it should be. I was told that I could go down in the tunnel that ran under the major halls of our building as he thought there were some math books being stored there. As to the type of math class, he said that he didn't care and was sure the students didn't either but to not teach what the other high school math teachers were teaching. A bit numb, I re-entered the classroom with my head swimming and continued the hour with current events, specifically relating math concepts. That afternoon, I found twenty-five long-forgotten, applied math books in the dank tunnel. Day three of the class, we began our semester of applied math in earnest.

I will say that I learned many, many things that semester: figuring board feet of lumber, measuring kilowatt hours, determining the amount of wood needed to build a house, how many gallons and how long it would take to fill a swimming pool given its dimensions, and other useful things. I could not imagine that happening in later years, but it did back in the day.

An Error in Judgment

I can distinctly remember the last time I saw this particular student. It was early in my teaching career. He was a seventh-grader of mine and had been absent for a few days. At that time, there was a one-way circle drive in front of the school, and the buses parked along the right side nearer the school to pick up and drop off students with the parents doing the same on the left side of the drive. It probably was not the safest arrangement because the students being picked up by their parents had to walk between the buses, but it wasn't a time when extreme measures to ensure safety were taken. People were expected to think, watch, and act with their own best interests in mind. My room faced this drive and the street beyond.

After being absent several days, maybe six, I saw the mom pull up mid-day and drop him off. He had come to pick up his homework that had been collected from his teachers earlier that morning. It was a blustery, rainy, November day. He wore jeans, a maroon sweatshirt, and a green Army parka popular in the day. The parka was open, flapping in the wind, as he entered the school to retrieve his missed work.

I distinctly remember thinking, "He certainly doesn't look very sick to me. He needs to be in school! We (the school personnel) are being taken for a ride."

A little more than three months later, I attended his funeral. His death had been the result of a type of childhood cancer, something I didn't imagine the day he came for his homework.

I still regret my snap judgment on that day long ago.

On Their Side

*I*n the summer of 1976, I took an assessment class primarily focusing on reading testing as I was earning my master's in secondary reading instruction. We were taught theory, test management, and the current assessments available the first two hours, and then students came for two hours so we could "practice" on them. After about the third week, the professor commented to me one day after class as I was packing my things, "You don't have very many discipline problems in your classroom, do you?" I had just finished my fourth year teaching and had not particularly thought about it. After thinking for a moment, I agreed and said that I did not have many. He then replied, "It is very easy for the kids to tell that you are on their side. They know you are working for them and genuinely like them." Throughout my career, I hoped that was always evident and true.

You Don't Have to Like Me

*N*ear the beginning of my teaching career (thankfully), I can remember telling classes, and believing, "I don't care if you like me; I just care if you learn the material." At the time, I thought I was being very practical and efficient and had little concern of what they thought of me.

In my naiveté, I failed to realize the chemistry that existed between people. If you didn't like someone, you were very unlikely to want to do your best in situations involving that person. Of course, I believed that we should all be self-oriented learners with lofty goals individualized unto ourselves, and still do to some extent, but realized that just didn't happen in the real world especially with those in junior high, or middle school as it became later known.

I now know if they liked me, they would follow my lead and great things could/would be accomplished. Did I care if they liked me? YES! Their liking me was directly related to their learning.

A Not-So-Proud Moment

*E*arly in my teaching career, I believed rules were rules and they were to be followed. Live with it.

Students did not leave my room for anything short of death, and I thought they could very likely stay for that, too.

Enter a tall, gangly, mother-raised, friendly, seventh-grader. He was always pleasant and sometimes did his work and sometimes didn't. He had lots of family issues and generally was kicked around by life but irrepressibly resilient.

One day, he asked if he could go to the bathroom. My thought was, "Over my dead body," but, "Of course not!" left my mouth. It wasn't long after his request, that I noticed a growing wet patch on his pants. The damage was done, and I was so sorry, which in no measure I am sure lessened his embarrassment. I have no idea how many others in the class, if any, had realized what had happened, but this was not a shining moment in my teaching career. Over twenty years have passed, and I still remember that incident with shame.

From that day forward, when asked, "May I go to the bathroom?" my response was always, "You bet!"

The Day the Helicopter Didn't Leave

*F*or seventeen years, I taught in the first room of the hall in which the principal's office was at the end. The hospital was across the drive to the north of the school. Across the street from the hospital to the east, there was an open field that was used by Flight Care to land the helicopter should a patient need to be transported to a larger, city hospital. My desk faced in that general direction with the students having it to their backs. But in saying that, the helicopter never landed and left without the students noticing with the noise and all.

Mid-morning one day, the helicopter came. As routine, the ambulance went down the hospital drive, across the street to the waiting helicopter, and the patient was loaded. The transfer area was far enough away that you couldn't identify the patient, but familiar team members or doctors could often be recognized. On that particular day, you could certainly tell what was happening as the event progressed. After the patient was loaded, the helicopter hovered about twenty feet above the ground ready to take off for the city. This day, it hovered there in mid-air for about ten minutes, not a good sign. I had come to learn that this meant that the medical team on board was trying to stabilize the patient.

That day, the hovering helicopter never left. After a few more than ten minutes, it settled to the ground. The patient was removed and placed back in the ambulance before being returned to the hospital. This usually signified the ending of a life.

We later learned that the patient was a former student in his early twenties. Being overwhelmed by life, he had used a gun and taken his life. I had not taught him but had his brother, and I would later have his sister.

I still remember the feeling of watching that helicopter hover and never leave, only to find out it was someone I knew. I remember that as one of the very saddest days of my career.

Another Sad Day

$\mathcal{I}$ had been at a meeting in the board room after school, so I was leaving about four o'clock, which was about thirty minutes later than my normal departure time. As I was walking to my car, I heard a siren wailing. The wind was blowing and the fastening rope of the flag was clanging against the pole as the flag blew in the breeze. I remember thinking, "I wonder if the ambulance is for someone I know?" And yes, the ambulance was for an eleventh-grade student who had a brain aneurysm and died. It was very sad, almost haunting, as I contemplated for whom the ambulance was. He had been one of mine. My heart is always sad and touched by the death of a former student.

Giving Up on Kids

When do you give up on kids? Never! Never! Never! If there's life, if there's breath, there is hope. However, I would give them (individually) my very best three motivational attempts. After giving them my three best shots possible, I'd let up a bit on my perpetual nagging. It was my thought that the student must step forward and show an inkling of interest, with my having given my level best for three times. I would beg, cajole, teach, reteach, and encourage. In fact, I never gave up encouraging. I gave a person three shots at being a good student, the student he or she could be. Then, if he or she were still completely resistant, I had to move on to the others.

I had as many as forty-three in my classes in my early years with the mid-thirties being the norm with respect to class size. Very simply, I needed to focus my energies on the rest of the class. I couldn't allow one or two to sap my energy that the others deserved. I let those who gave up be whatever it was they chose to be as long as it didn't interfere with the class.

Oh, I assigned lunch study, recommended after-school study, and used the mechanisms in place for such happenings most certainly, and continued to care, ever offering encouraging words. But I simply couldn't invest my whole heart in a student after three of my very best attempts to reach him or her. I simply didn't have the energy or the time to continue in full-forced nagging mode and be fair to the others in the class.

After all, I had an equal responsibility to every other student in the classroom. However, if a student would turn to the light, so to speak, ask a question, or at all show a glimmer of interest, I would once again be right there for him or her. That meant the student was back in the game, and we would become intensely engaged in a teacher-student relationship.

A File of Names

One thing I would suggest to beginning teachers is to keep on file (electronic or otherwise) a record of each student taught, the year, grade, and subject. I thought of this during my third year of teaching and had the erroneous thought that it was too late to start. I can't tell you how many times I wished I had a list of those students. In saying that, I do think it would be less important if you didn't stay in the same district for your entire career.

Setting Standards

I pretty much had a rule during my years of teaching that I wouldn't do in front of the class what I wouldn't allow my students to do. If I wouldn't let them have anything to drink, then I shouldn't have anything to drink. I always felt that I should hold myself to the same standard or higher to which I held them. In later years after the brain research was done, water was always acceptable in my room for them or for me. In saying that, I'm not talking flavored water, juice, or pop – just plain water.

Occasionally, I would bend the rules for them and for me if an extenuating circumstance existed. But I feel very strongly to be respected, honored, and thought of as fair, I had to live by the standards I imposed upon them. Not only did I have to live by those standards, but I needed to be the exemplar, or standard bearer. I stand by that. If it were a rule for them, it was a rule for me. Over time, that attitude built big dividends in credibility.

How Much Do They Care?

*W*hen I began teaching, I had the feeling that the students didn't care as much as we did when I was in school, just a few, short years prior to that, especially about their goals and their thoughts of what teachers had to say. I felt as though they were thinking themselves more sophisticated and less interested in what teachers had to offer them. Over the years, I have found that to be so untrue. The longer I taught, the more I realized how much the students cared. Oh, they may not have looked like it at the time, and they may not have sat there and said, "I'm hanging on your every word," but in truth many times, they were. I think this was brought home to me in two instances I remember distinctly, both very poignant examples.

The first one I remember relates to a time that I had taught a sister and a brother both of whom were very nice, cooperative, and friendly. The sister was older by several years. A couple of years after I had taught the brother, he died in an accidental shooting incident. Another teacher and I went to the funeral home to offer our sympathy to the family. We talked with the parents. Over at the side, the sister was standing. We went to her, as she came to us. She thanked us for coming. I expressed how very, very sorry I was about her brother's death. At this very poignant, sad time in her life she looked at me and said, "Mrs. Hile, may I tell you what I am doing?"

"Well, of course, I'd love to know," was my response.

She then said very proudly, "I'm a science teacher, just like you, only I have ninth-graders." Not only was I proud of her, but it made me realize just how much I mattered to her. In this sad time, when her mind was on so many things, she wanted me, her junior high science teacher, to know what she had done with her life. I felt deeply honored.

Then another time, there was a family that I had taught probably three of their four children and one boy in both junior high and high school. They were a lovely family with fun kids; I always got along with them really well. The son, who I had taught both in junior high and high school, had married, had a child, divorced, and moved to another part of the country. His son remained with his mother and attended our school. Sadly, when his son was in sixth grade, he was tragically killed in a car accident on a stormy winter's night. He had been in the classroom just across the hall. Of course, I went to the funeral home. Now, understand that I hadn't seen the father for many, many years, possibly as many as twenty-five. I had known and taught the mother, too. When I arrived at the visitation, they had separate lines visiting with those who had come offering their sympathy. All was very amicable. After talking to the mother and offering my sympathy, I went to the father's line and waited respectfully back from where he was talking to another. Then, it became my turn to talk to the dad. He looked up with a, "Who's next?" inquiry on his face. With that look, I realized that he didn't recognize me. I would like to think that it was just my different hair style, as I changed often in those days. As I stepped forward, I said softly, "Hello," using his name.

To that opening, he immediately responded as he recognized my voice, "Oh hello, Mrs. Hile!" coming forward and tightly hugging me. As we were talking, he told me that he had hoped his son would have me as a teacher in the coming years and that he had told him all about me. He then said with his arm around me, "Mrs. Hile, I want you to know that I made something of myself. I graduated from (*a notable college out East*) with a B+ average. I did it." Now here was a man at the funeral home visitation for his son, at this time of extreme grief that I can't imagine, wanting me to know that he had made something of himself and had graduated from college with a B+ average. Remember, it had been well over twenty years since I had seen him.

Students care! Oh, they care so very much, and we need to always remember how very much they care whether their caring is obvious or not. As teachers, we need to remember that every day when we walk into the classroom that we are making memories for them. We are giving legs to their dreams. We will be people they remember far into the future; may it be with a smile in their hearts as someone who made a positive difference in their lives.

A Ditzy Parent a Ditzy Child Does Not Make

I can think of two seventh-grade girls who were probably the most ditzy girls I have ever taught. Oh, they were very pleasant and friendly. Both were very chatty, usually not about class material. They looked around them with an expression of a chicken just hatched from the egg unsure of what was happening. I remember wondering about each with trepidation, "What will ever happen to her in this world?"

Well, many years down the road, and this is one of the benefits of teaching in the same school system for your career, I taught their children. Both had a son and a daughter. I taught both of one family and the girl of the other. I can assure you that the children of these space cadets (nice, but nevertheless space cadets) were terrific, appropriately mature, and engaged students.

Oh yes, they do grow up! Anything's possible. As I said, when I had these two women as seventh-grade girls, I wondered what would ever become of them. Well, what became of them was that they grew up. They became wonderful community members, wives, parents, and professional workers. Now, it seems amazing to me I would have ever doubted that outcome.

Having Taught the Parents

To my knowledge, I didn't teach any third generations, but I do know they were "out there" and of an age that I could have. Maybe I have without realizing it, but no one mentioned it to me. As of my last year teaching, for about 60 percent of my students, I had taught one or both parents. I absolutely loved that fact. It made classroom discipline a no-brainer. Also, they came to my class knowing that I valued their doing the assigned work and had expectations that they do just that with consequences if they didn't. After all, their parents had lived through having me as a teacher, they could/would, too.

Once early in the school year when assigning lunch study to a student who hadn't completed his assignment, he said with a wry smile on his face, "My dad said this would happen." Yep, it happened. In his father's day, it was an after-school assigned time, but the same principle was in effect: there are consequences if you do not do your school work.

I have never found that having taught the parent or parents worked against me. I felt it always worked for me. There was a respect, a bond, a built-in familiarity that existed. I didn't get questioned like the newer teachers. I didn't get caught under fire. I had the students' respect and support from the first day of class. I was not starting at square one with them. I had a track record, which most often was favorable and reaped positive benefits. Having students of parents I had taught was an absolute joy!

Sometimes, I thought that they behaved well just because they thought that if they didn't, I'd "poof" into a pile of dirt on the floor being that ancient. After all, I had their parents; I must be really old. If for nothing more than that reason, they treated me kindly, not wanting to add to my demise and having to explain that to anyone.

In truth, I would tell them that I loved having had their parents and now them. Yes, it meant that I was old, but I'd be old anyway. I might as well be old and have them!

Many times, it was, "Aha, so that was your dad or mother!" explaining so very much to me about the child just knowing that fact.

It has been my privilege to witness and teach the different generations, a great joy!

Pass on the Good

I love plays, especially Broadway musicals. I have season tickets to three different venues, traveling regularly as far as one hundred miles to attend. Not too long ago, I was sitting in the 2,500 seat Great Hall of Wharton Center on the campus of

Michigan State University. When there, I usually do not see people I know; on occasion I have, but normally not. That particular evening at intermission, I heard, "Mrs. Hile, Mrs. Hile," and one of my former students was standing there behind me. Not only had she been a former student, but so had her mother, father, and older brother who graduated with my older son. As we talked, I learned that she was a police officer with three children and lived in the area. She was attending the play with her sister.

She was absolutely delighted to see me. Former students have no idea what it means for them to come and to recognize me, saying "Hello" with friendliness. We spent a year of our lives together, and they are so welcoming. I would encourage anyone to say "Hi" to his or her former teachers if the opportunity presents itself. I would also say that if you have a special teacher or teachers, go out of your way to write them a note or give them a call. Maybe just, "I was thinking about you today, and it has been fifteen years (or whatever) since I had you. I would just like you to know…" I will guarantee you that not only will you make that teacher's day and month, but very possibly you will be making that person's entire year! It's happened to me. I have had students contact me on a few occasions after many years, thanking me for really just doing my job. What a thrill it was! Pass on the good.

Shades of the Past

$\mathscr{T}$here were so many benefits of teaching in the same school for a significant span of years besides it being just plain fun. A few years before retiring in the spring while attending an IEP (Individualized Educational Plan) to select high school classes for a student, I strongly felt that the high school special education teacher representative was familiar. I did not recognize her name as being from our area. While others were talking and papers were being signed, I sidled to the person next to me and asked if the high school teacher had gone to our school. The answer was, "No, I don't think so." Being overheard by the assistant principal, he quietly added that he thought her mother had been a student of ours. That suggestion was all it took to activate my mind. I spun around, looked at the teacher, and said when it seemed appropriate, "Was your mother (*Name*)?" Yes, indeed she was. I had taught this woman's mother in junior high and in high school and always thought of her with high regard. The teacher, in fact, had been seen by me many, many years ago probably when she was about four years old riding in a shopping cart while her mother was grocery shopping. Her mother and I chatted as she played in the cart. Now, here she was a colleague who interestingly lived one and a half miles north of me. I found that connection amazing!

It also needs to be said that one of the supreme joys of my teaching career for me was to have former students as colleagues. I thrilled to see them taking their places within our school structure and excelling. In addition to it suggesting that we/I hadn't damaged them too badly, it also suggested we may have actually done something right. In my last year of teaching, five of the teachers with whom I worked closely in our building had been my students. It was a wonderful feeling working with them.

Parent Support

A few years ago while attending an event in a neighboring county, I was approached by a former student whom I had taught early in my career. More recently, I taught his son. His daughter attended our school but had not been one of my students, but I did know her to be delightful. All to say, it was more than good to see this man. He was very friendly and acted genuinely happy to see me.

Let me tell you about his son. He came to eighth grade, and the parents requested a staff meeting the first week of school. They told all of us, his teachers, that their son had profound ADHD. However, they only wanted to make us aware of that fact. They believed if he were to be successful in life that he, with their and our help, would have to develop coping strategies. They wanted us to know that they would try their very best to get and keep him organized and support him in any way they could. They also told us, and I remember this specifically, that if their son left a book at school that he needed, one of them would drive him back to school (as they lived a few miles in the country), knock on the doors until a custodian came, and have him get the forgotten book from his locker so he could do his homework and have it completed on time. They wanted us to help keep their son organized in any way that we could, but the onus was clearly on their son, no question there. That day we were being informed of their acknowledgement of their son's defined disability, their commitment to him developing coping skills, the enlisting of our cooperation, and their earnest desire for him to learn as much and as well as he could. They were totally supportive of his teachers and also wanted us to have the highest expectations for their son.

Many parents would have requested the meeting and told us not to expect as much of their child because of the ADHD, using it as an excuse. Not these folks. Their son did extremely well in eighth grade, receiving many awards at the end of the year. Four years later, he graduated at the top of his class, attended a major university earning advanced degrees, and now is happily practicing in his profession. Those parents very well understood what was possible for their son, fueled his dreams, and were willing to give him the support to make them happen. I honor and celebrate their success and all of the families who do the same.

Are Kids Different Today?

*Y*es, I thought that once. They are certainly growing up in a different world with the Internet, social networking, different world situations, and instant communications. But each generation has its special situations in the world and unique set of circumstances like none other before it or to come. After thirty-eight years of teaching, I have come to believe the kids are pretty much the same. Kids want structure whether they admit it or not. Kids are apprehensive about their futures and want guidance. Kids want rules. If you show them what you expect, more often than not they are going to achieve it.

I have come to learn that if you do those things, you will be well remembered by them. Throughout my teaching career and in my life today, whether buying popcorn at the show, shopping in Walmart, or being in just about at any public venue, a former student will remind me of something I did or have said. These are often people now in their forties. I laugh at what they remember, things long forgotten by me, but they usually sound like something I would have said or done. We as teachers must always remember we are important to them, many, many of them, and that sometimes we were the very best part of their day.

I do think in my fifty-five years spent in public education as a student and a teacher that involvement from the home has somewhat eroded. Of course, the family structure has seen more stress in recent years with both parents needing to work and a variety of living arrangements. I am of the Baby Boomer Generation with parents who were often deprived of an education. My parents' stance was that the school was right, even when the school may have been wrong on a rare occasion. It was very well understood when I left home in the morning that if I were disciplined at school, I would receive much more severe consequences at home that evening. The school was right, right or wrong. For them, it was that simple. That isn't the case so much anymore, and I'm not sure that's all bad.

As far as the kids being different from years past, they do come from a variety of backgrounds, ethnic groups, races, religions, socio-economic groups, and other demographics more so than in the past. I remember in my elementary school class of about thirty-four students back in the mid-1950s that there was only one other student who had divorced parents. We were the only two in the class, and some students were instructed by their parents not to play with us because of that fact. Of course, that is no longer the case. If I were guessing, less than half of my students in my later years of teaching came from traditional, two-parent households living with both of their biological parents. The times have changed with so many different and creative living arrangements.

Back to the question: are the kids different today? They certainly do live in a different world, but as I stated at the beginning: I am not so sure that they are all that different from previous generations. Their circumstances are, yes. The kids? I don't think so.

The Power of Our Words

*I*n planning special education students' schedules in preparation for high school, I was often included in the meetings as a general education teacher. I always welcomed these opportunities to assist in assuring the best possible placement for the students as they began their high school careers.

Several years ago, I was invited to an IEP (Individualized Educational Plan) meeting for a student I had in eighth grade. I had taught this girl's mother several years prior to having her. The meeting had begun when I arrived as I had to wait for the roving sub to cover my classroom. Almost immediately upon my arrival, the administrator overseeing the meeting turned to me and asked my assessment of the student. I told the group that I found her delightful, hard working, and always pleasant, and I was sure with her good work ethic and the proper scheduling that she would be fine, do well even, in high school. After making my comments, I returned to class.

Later that spring at a graduation open house at which her parents were also attending, the mother came over to me and said that she wanted to thank me. I looked at her blankly. She went on to say that the IEP for her daughter was not going well before I arrived. She stated that they were being told about her daughter's deficiencies and inadequacies with a bleak outlook for her high school future. The mother told me that when I entered and made my positive statements, the entire mood of the meeting shifted and that after I left, they focused on what her daughter could do and, building on her strengths, made appropriate selections for her high school classes. She said that my coming to the meeting was like a breath of fresh air and that what I had to say changed everything. She was very, very grateful for my words.

Not too long ago, I saw the mother and asked how "our girl" was doing. She told me that her daughter had graduated from college and was working in a job she loved having just purchased her own home. Of course, I was delighted. Our eyes met and held for a few "knowing" moments, and she again said, "Thank you, Mrs. Hile." I think we rarely realize the power of our words.

My Most Treasured Compliments

*O*f all of the compliments that I have received, I especially treasure the ones in which the student tells me that he or she didn't like the subject (usually science) but now absolutely loves it.

But even more prized than that, the ultimate thrill for me is when the student says, "I didn't think that I could do it, but you made me believe that I could." To me, there is no higher compliment from a student: "You made me believe that I could do this. Your belief in me made me want to achieve, and I did."

I was very ill during my next to last year of teaching, being hospitalized in critical care for a week, and missing three and a half weeks of school. During my illness and absence from school, I received so many lovely cards from my students. Yes, I received the large sheets on which they all signed their names, too. But many, many took the time to individually send me a card and note. I treasured each and every contact from my students. As I mentioned previously, I think the highest compliments I have ever had are when I am told by the students that they didn't believe they could succeed, and I made them believe that they could. Of course, it is only my encouragement; they, in truth, did the work. It gave me great delight to "plant" that idea for them, holding out the possibility of their success; it's simply part of what a teacher does.

Catching a Dream

I often wondered if any of my middle school students knew, realized, cared, or ever contemplated the adult life they would like to live. I did have one girl who, for the record, announced during class that she would like to either be the leader of the apocalypse or an ultrasound technician. Ignoring the leader of the apocalypse comment, I suggested that before she became an ultrasound technician that I was pretty sure she needed to pass eighth grade, something very doubtful at least at that point in the school year. That thought had not apparently occurred to her as she seemed rather stunned.

I do know you can live the life of your dreams, the one you've imagined, because I am doing so. I also know it takes vision, thought, consistent choices with that end in mind, and lots of hard work. I would be the first to say it is worth every bit of the effort required. I have become the person I wanted to be. Of course, life is not stagnant, and I now have new hopes and dreams of a continued future. Life moves forward.

I always wanted my students to know that having the life of their dreams was possible.

Where Teachers Spend Their Time

$\mathcal{W}$here do teachers spend their time? Because they teach, they live in the future. Most of their "products" will never be seen by them.

The middle school students come into the classroom short, tall, in-between, bright, dull, eager, and lethargic. They are the adolescents of today, as many and varied as the stars.

The students come with their hopes and dreams – and sometimes with no hopes and dreams.

Teachers are in the business of getting them ready for the world, ensuring that they have a wonderful and bright future!

The Rat

*O*ne mid-winter day, my first hour, science class was working at the counters on an assignment. I looked up from my desk to see a foot long, brown rat ambling down the aisle between the second and third rows. I assumed it had somehow come in from the cold by the poorly insulated, very drafty heat conduits under the windows, finding an opening large enough to allow its wiggling entry. I quietly told my cadet to go get the custodian!

Meanwhile, I calmly (like any good science teacher) told the students that we had a visitor and to remain at their stations. Several gasped, others' eyes popped open like sewer lids, and all except one remained in place exactly as I had asked. This boy was walking toward the rat. I loudly restated that everyone should remain where they were. He, a normally cooperative, nice kid, kept walking toward the rat. Then, I pointed my finger and screamed at him, "Stay where you are!" as I continued to gaze at the rat. He took another step forward. I just could not figure out why this normally congenial boy was being so defiant of my direct order, especially under these unusual circumstances. I was about to yell again, when I looked at his face. "Oh," I said, "you two know each other." He then slinked to the rat noticeably relieved, picked it up, and went to his seat before I sent him to the office. It seems his pet rat had unexpectedly hitched a ride to school in his backpack.

The office secretary later told me that after I had sent him from class to the office that he had stood at her desk opposite her with his hands behind his back. When she questioned him, he told her that Mrs. Hile had "kicked him out" of class. This rather surprised the secretary as I very rarely sent students to the office for discipline, especially one as mild-mannered and nice as this young man. When she inquired as to specifically why I had sent him, he plopped the rat on her blotter. Immediately, she understood. I was told that while he waited for his mother to come to retrieve his rat that he sat in the principal's office with it cozily wrapped around his neck.

There was never a dull moment teaching middle school.

Throwing Up

*F*or many, many years I wondered why teachers had students who vomited in their classrooms. Didn't they let them leave? Who would keep a kid who was sick? I thought it entirely preventable; move them right out the door upon discovering any problem. The hall was fair game and not particularly "on our watch." Then, along came teaching year number twenty-eight. I heard an odd noise, looked up, and three seats back in the second row a student had begun hurling (best descriptive word possible for the event). This student spewed and sprayed everyone within six feet and even some three rows from the event. From that day, I understood that sometimes a student will vomit in class.

Mixed Memories of Events that Did and Didn't Happen

I've come to think that many students don't remember too much of anything specific that was taught in middle school; of course, some do. Some will see me at the show or in the grocery store and say, "Mrs. Hile you taught me…," or "You said…" I smile as it usually sounds like me. Did I or did I not? Sometimes, I'm not sure.

I remember being at a funeral home visitation of the grandmother of someone I taught long ago. He had become a doctor and was well into his forties. He introduced me to his wife whom I had never met. Then he went on to say, "I'll never forget in eighth-grade life science, you took two poisonous substances and made something we could eat. You took hydrochloric acid and sodium hydroxide, put them together and made salt. I will never forget that day!" A lifelong memory was made on that day so very long ago.

On the other hand, not too long ago, we had someone working in the cafeteria that I had taught in eighth grade. I said, "Glad to see you; it's always good to see former students working here." I also had taught his father and had his brother that year, so I was very familiar with the family.

He said with a big grin, "Oh, good to see you, too, Mrs. Hile. I'll never forget when we made the hot air balloons in your class, and one got stuck on the school roof almost burning down the school!"

I laughed and said, "Are you sure that was my class?" He assured me that it was, stating that he remembered it as if it were yesterday.

I smiled and said, "Luckily, we saved the school." In truth, it was a high school class in which he had made the hot air balloon, not mine. That teacher and I had a lot of similarities, being of the same age, build, and hair color. Obviously, two of his former science teachers had melded and switched in his mind.

Another former junior high student in his forties adamantly averred during a graduation gathering that he had me for eighth-grade science, when my teaching partner and I both knew full well that he had her.

Sometimes students tell me things that happened, and I know very well they didn't – at least not in my classroom. On many occasions, it's not my faulty memory, it is theirs. I think it's always interesting when you have students tell you of things that happened in your class long ago, and you know that they have it confused with another school experience. I always liked the saying that I had on a card I picked up at an in-service intended for the parents that read, "If you will promise not to believe everything your child says happens at school, I will promise not to believe everything he or she says happens at home." Mixed memories are amazing things, in truth, probably theirs and mine.

Making Better Choices

I hear people talk about the students of today and how awful they are and not like the students used to be. You know what? We had kids in trouble when I went to school over fifty years ago. I'm not going to tell you there aren't kids in trouble today, because there are. But I don't see a vast increase over what there has ever been. Most of the kids I taught were absolutely wonderful. They were kids; thirteen- and fourteen-year-old students for the most part. They were not thirty-five-year-old, seasoned adults. Yes, from time to time they made poor choices. If so, I told them to make better choices in the future. In my opinion, that's what growing up is all about: making better choices. I would tell them that I was an old lady, and I still made some poor choices. What that meant was next time I would consciously try to make a better choice. I was a work in progress, too.

I had and have faith in the future of this country, primarily because I have faith in its kids.

A few summers ago, some friends and I had lunch in Harbor Springs, a beautiful, vacation town on the water of Michigan's northern Lake Michigan shore. We dined inside, but when we left we had to walk by outside tables. I overheard one lady telling another that the kids today just didn't have any respect and how awful they were, not knowing what was going to happen to the children of today. My friend slipped her arm in mine, tightened her grip, and said, "Just keep walking; we don't have time for you to tell them differently." How very well she knew me.

Front-Loading

I truly believe you will have a more successful year teaching if you front-load. To me, that means you work twenty-six hours a day at the start of the school year. You scramble setting everything in motion and plan for every conceivable outcome. Then you work very, very hard to make sure everything unfolds correctly. You *tell* them what you expect of them; you *show* them; and you are *actively involved* in making it happen. This takes a lot of energy but it pays off big time with the rewards being significant as the year progresses.

If you do a really good job of front-loading by setting your expectations, making the students understand, adjusting when needed, and being consistent, by mid-October you can have a life again, and the year will almost seemingly effortlessly run smoothly. Never underestimate the value of front-loading. Get the job done right at the beginning and work from a position of confidence that you have done all you can, not one of "let's see if this is enough," adding improvements as you go. At the year's beginning, set high standards, create the habits, follow them consistently, leave nothing to chance, and you *will* have a wonderful year.

Calling Home for the Top Student in Each Class

$\int$omething I did the last two years of my teaching career was calling the parents of the top-scoring, academic student in each of my classes at the end of figuring grades for the week and congratulating them. The grades were available online to the families, but they didn't know how their son or daughter compared to the others in the class. So, I would call and very enthusiastically say something like, "Hi, this is Mrs. Hile, (*name of child's*) teacher. I'd like you to know that your child has the top grade in my "whatever" hour "whatever" class. Congratulations to you, the parents, for your support and making this possible! I just wanted to let you know how well he/she was doing and thank you. Be sure to tell him/her I called."

First of all, the parent was delighted to receive a call from school that wasn't complaining. They were genuinely thrilled. And yes, sometimes it was the same student's family that I called week after week for a particular hour, eventually memorizing the phone number. To those, I would sometimes joke with the opening remark, "Hi, Mrs. Hile, your friendly phone stalker..." before continuing with my conversation. I never sensed that with the repeated calls anyone ever felt the least bit inconvenienced. They all welcomed my calls. Some classes had the top four or five students in fierce competition to receive "the call" for the week.

This act of recognizing students for their excellence was a very positive thing and simple to do. I only wish that I would have thought of it sooner in my career.

Positive Compliments

I always tried to find what the students were doing right and compliment it, rather than jumping in and correcting some perceived "wrong" behavior. However, in saying that, there were times that I needed to jump in or someone might have been hurt. From my own experience, I know that I tried to honor any compliment given to me by trying to live up to the expectation the person had of me. If someone were telling me what was wrong, I felt less likely to want to excel in his or her presence; rather, I'd walk on egg shells just doing enough to get by without retribution and recrimination. But given someone who believed in me and tossed me a compliment, I would try to fly to the moon if needed.

Personal Comments

I found mentioning something personal to my students, non-school related, went a long way in having them see me as a person and not just "the teacher." I often commented about their clothes, matching colors, jewelry, hair styles, performance at an athletic, band, or choir event, or whatever just so they knew I saw them as people first, students second.

Planting Seeds

I never knew how a suggestion or casual comment would come to fruition. I liked to think of myself as a person of action, and planting seeds seemed a slow way to a desired outcome. However, I have seen mountains moved from the tiniest seed. Most times the transformation in thinking was not readily apparent, but down the road given time, the seeds flourished and took hold. I felt, and still feel, those in education needed to continually keep planting seeds. When the conditions were right, mighty things happened.

Perspective

*L*ong ago while teaching seventh-grade reading and spelling exclusively, which I did for five years, picking up science again in 1984, I came to realize the way I viewed my students had a lot more to do with me than them. I had a book report due each marking period. Being ever organized, the book reports were due the week before the marking period's end, giving me ample correcting time. My general attitude about my students the Friday I collected the book reports was one of mild disdain. I felt they were careless, sloppy, and generally not very nice. The correcting of the book reports loomed menacing my weekend, and I was always a bit cranky spending most of the following Sunday correcting into the late night. Those were the days of thirty students per class as the norm and sometimes as many as thirty-six, so 150 book reports were "usual."

Then, almost as if by magic, with my Parker, medium, blue pen making the last stroke on the then completed stack, my attitude shifted. Suddenly, my students were wonderful, caring, bright, witty, and interested. These were the very same students I had left on Friday having less than a positive assessment, and now on Sunday night having their book reports corrected I was willing to embrace their innate worth and defend them to anyone. You see the cause of the change was not they. It was I. I was out from under the correcting pile, and my attitude had improved significantly. Over the years when I would become "down on" my students, I learned to look inward, and more times than not, I found it was something happening with me and not related to them at all.

Similarly, in March I thought I needed to have my head examined for being a teacher. The rest of the year, I thought it was the greatest job on the planet, and I was delighted to have spent most of my professional career teaching seventh- and eighth-graders. I learned it was all perspective.

Courtesy, Courtesy, Courtesy

$\mathscr{I}$ would like to think that I have always been respectful to kids, but in the summer of 1988, I took ITIP (Instructional Theory into Practice) developed by Madelyn Hunter. By that time, I had been teaching many years. That workshop taught a rather novel concept, at least to me at the time: thanking kids for doing things, everyday classroom things. Thanking them for passing up their papers was one example suggested to the members of the workshop. Recognizing them for doing well and being courteous to them were two other tenants taught. I would like to think that I had always treated my students with dignity, but that workshop opened my eyes. I went back to school after that summer and started to thank my students for passing up their papers, sliding their chairs under their desks, picking up papers, or whatever. "Pass your papers up, please. Thank you. Thank you. Pass your folders to the front. Thank you. Thank you." I would have been the first to admit that it sounded hokey to me at first, thanking them for something that was accepted as good student behavior and expected. After a while, it felt less hokey. It became absolutely amazing the effect it had upon them. Over the years, it developed into my unconscious competence becoming second nature and a very real part of me and my teaching. It probably took a year or two for it to become automatic. In later years, it freely rolled off of my lips whenever my students did any little thing for me. "Thank you," said earnestly and related to a specific event became my standard.

I have had several students comment since doing this, especially those seated near the front of the class handing me the collected papers, "You always say thank you to us. You're always so polite to us."

"Well, I should be; you're polite to me," became my usual response. Truly, they were. I do know there were things they would do/pull in other classes that they flat out would be embarrassed to pull in front of me; they simply wouldn't dream of doing some of their outrageous stunts in my class. I believe part of that was because I always treated them with courtesy and respect, and in doing so, expected to be treated well by them. It was a two-way street. Rarely, have I been disappointed, and those times were usually followed by an apology, if somewhat later in coming. I think the students were and are amazing and did and will most times rise to your expectations. Treat them well.

Constructive Criticism

$\mathcal{I}$ have come to believe that there is no such thing as constructive criticism. Criticism is criticism. That is not to say that teachers should not point out areas in which students are in error and build on them. But to think that criticism is the only route, I have come to realize, is very short-sighted. It's suggesting an extremely small bag of tricks.

Think of your own life. When someone gave you a compliment, how did you want to present yourself to him or her the next time you met? You wanted to at least meet the expectations the person had of you and most times exceed them. You desired to rise to those perceived expectations. If someone were routinely telling you what was wrong with what you were doing, you'd usually have that pit in your stomach when confronted by him or her again that said, "Oh, what's wrong now?" You would have been making adjustments from a feeling of trepidation and dread, not one of joy. I thought that was not what I wanted to do as a teacher.

I have learned, and oh have I learned over the years at the cost of many students I am sure, to always tell the students what they are doing right. I tried to celebrate their successes. At times, I would possibly make a subtle suggestion that something may have been improved, but found they could usually figure that out for themselves. By giving them the confidence on which to build, amazing things happened.

So, as far as constructive criticism and feeling that I had the obligation to tell them what was wrong, I tried very hard to stay in the land of the positive. When they hadn't reached the goal, correction was done with gentleness and an encouraging manner, celebrating the aspects that were met. I found that in consistently showing them what they were doing right, they wanted to do right more, and did.

Be Ridiculous

$\mathcal{I}$ am not sure this would apply to all age groups, but it most certainly suited middle school students. I was ridiculous, and they loved it. Of course, wisely I had established my credibility and authority over the years. Each student knew I was a long-time, well-established professional.

When teaching genetics the first day, I would dress in my husband's long, brown bathrobe as Gregor Mendel from the mid-1800s Austria. Immediately after the bell, I would burst through the prep room door staggering pretending to be lost in time and expecting it to be my physics classroom in nineteenth-century Austria. I'd even use a hokey European accent. I feigned amazement to be in an unexpected place. After eliciting from them where and what the class was, I told them since I was already there I might as well teach them some genetics, being known as *The Father of Genetics* and all. How fortuitous it was that we had connected in time!

One day after my Gregor Mendel stint on the first day of the semester, I went to my teaching partner's room. It was my conference period and her students were entering. A girl who had just come from my genetics class arrived and when she saw me announced to anyone willing to listen that they didn't have Mrs. Hile last hour because Gregor Mendel came instead. Before the class began, I asked her some eight or ten questions pertaining to what Gregor Mendel had told them. She knew every single answer, and another student who had been there began chiming in correct comments as well while she was being quizzed. I delighted at the information retained.

Whenever I was goofy, it was like I was on the kids' side. They loved it, and more importantly, they remembered.

Reading with Panache

$\mathcal{S}$etting the stage for what was to be studied, I always read the chapter previews (usually a page) orally in my science classes. I read with great enthusiasm and gusto, complete with highly exaggerated sound effects employing onomatopoeia to the max. They loved it; I loved it; everybody was happy. Moreover, they were engaged in the reading, anticipating the material to come.

Words of Wisdom

Interspersed during the hour, I regularly gave my students Words of Wisdom, which I called "WOW" for each assignment or whenever I thought they needed to know something. I would tell them what to look for, the pitfalls to avoid, how to most successfully proceed, etc. They knew when I blared, "WOW!" to listen, as they would be getting pertinent information about the task at hand: Words of Wisdom, aka WOW.

Puzzles

I have always enjoyed puzzles. For many years, I had a puzzle hanging in a designated area of my classroom. The first student or group of students to answer the puzzle correctly each hour received five bonus points, small when you considered that I had 1,200 plus points each marking period. I posted a new puzzle each Monday or the day after each hour successfully solved it, whichever came first. Some students were avid solvers, and others barely knew it was in the room. In a few cases, students would spend so much time trying to solve the puzzle that I felt they might have been a tad distracted from their assignments with that being a definite down side. Happily, those cases were few. Over the years, many enjoyed the puzzles and eagerly looked forward to rushing into the room trying to be the first to solve them, creating a positive, learning climate.

Behavior Reward Sheets

*L*ong ago, I realized that something should be done for those students who routinely, day in and day out, did exactly what was expected. I kept meticulous records and liked so doing. I would jokingly tell my students that I even wrote down if they were breathing. Once into the school year, I awarded a Behavior Reward Sheet to those students who had all of their work completed on time, been in class on time with their materials, had not left for the bathroom, and had not been spoken to concerning their behavior for two weeks. Ideally, this would be awarded after any ten-day-stretch of compliance. In reality, I determined the recipients at the end of each week. In doing so, if they "messed up" they didn't have to wait a complete two-week cycle to begin counting to be again eligible. The slips were worth ten points on any daily assignment and could be used at any time either with the assignment when due or retroactively any time prior to the marking period's end. Multiple slips could be used on an assignment. In truth, it was a point a day. "Big whoop," you may say; however, the students groveled for them. The slip was a way of recognizing their faithfulness to the task and, in time, added up to a nice grade improvement, even substantial at times. The students quite literally beamed when given one. I also made sure I was seen distributing them with fanfare each Monday and did not just slip them in their folders. I wanted them to be noticed for their positive efforts and desired actions.

Sample...

$Date$ _____

This is to tell the world that _____
has had excellent classroom conduct and has completed all of his/her assignments on time for two weeks in Mrs. Hile's class. This award may be exchanged for 10 points on any daily assignment. The points given for any assignment may not exceed the total possible. Some restrictions may apply. No expiration date.

Mrs. Michele Hile

Continued Encouragement

*T*he first day back after spring break, I gave to each student the following handout and spoke to the whole class about it. I assured them this was exactly how I felt and wanted them to have it stated in writing. I printed it on pastel paper significant of spring.

We are at the beginning of the end of the school year. Things will go very quickly these next few weeks, and I do not want the school year to end without you. Please know, I have thoroughly enjoyed having you in class and being your teacher, and there is no place else I would rather be for now than here in this room as your teacher. To ensure a successful end to the school year, I want you to commit yourself to continued excellence by being engaged and doing all of the assignments completely and carefully. If you haven't been terribly engaged, start now: it is not too late. I believe in your ability to succeed. May this final time together help well prepare you for your future years of education and life. Remember what Eleanor Roosevelt said, "The future belongs to those who believe in the beauty of their dreams." Believe in your dreams! Keep working and stay the course.

Educationally yours,

Michele Hile ☺

Teachers Have a Common Bond

*I*n my life as an ordained minister, I travel across the country officiating weddings. Many times my husband will travel with me, but often he does not. One summer, I officiated a yard wedding in a town about forty miles from our home. My husband did not travel with me. These were people I did not know, but after meeting with the bride and groom, writing their ceremony, and overseeing the rehearsal, I had a flavor for both families. When it came time for the reception at a lovely hall, I found myself seated with the groom's aunts and uncles and their children, almost all of whom were teachers. Going around our table, the girl to my immediate right had just graduated from college with her teaching degree and was job hunting; her mother was a teacher of over thirty years; her father was a retired teacher of thirty-three years; his sister was a former teacher now working in cancer research; her husband was a teacher; as were their son and his wife. The next table was an extension of that family and several were teachers, too. All to say, I was in very good company and there was a common bond.

They were sitting down for dinner with the minister, me, and didn't know me from Adam. I introduced myself and began talking to the girl beside me, who had just graduated from college and was looking for a teaching job. I wished her well and mentioned that I had just retired from teaching middle school for thirty-eight years. Wow, that's all it took! The others caught threads of the conversation, and asked, "You were a teacher?"

"Well, I was, but as of July 1, I am retired," I responded. We all shared our experiences, and we immediately hit it off sharing that common ground. I was no longer among strangers, the groom's family, but rather among friends, if unknown, fellow teachers. Playful kidding, jokes, and a happy attitude prevailed. Let's face it, we shared a common experience; we'd been on the line every day teaching kids, understanding one another's life motivation.

We were eating and the father looked up at me and said, "How come they didn't have you do a blessing? They should have had you do that before we ate."

I smiled, and the rest of the table chimed in with, "Well, she did." He responded that it must have been when he had stepped out to the restroom. His wife and daughter informed him that he was, indeed, right in his seat while I said grace.

I then playfully said to him, "Remember that time when it became really quiet and you were wondering what they were going to serve for dinner? That was probably the prayer." It was a smart aleck remark, but offered with a smile. We all burst out laughing, the father included. I could do that because I knew their senses of humor; I knew their experiences; we were brothers and sisters at heart; we were teachers.

I Teach Because...

*S*everal years ago (probably in the mid '80s), I put on my wall above the white board near my desk the sentence starter, "I teach because..." and followed it by six endings.

"I teach because... it's fun; ...I like school; ...I enjoy learning; ...I want the best possible life for you; ...my teachers believed in me; ...I believe in YOU!"

I stood by those statements.

The last few years I taught, I had beside the quote an 8" x 10" picture each of my ninth-grade civics teacher, Gladys Wiltse, and tenth-grade biology teacher, Suzanne Harwick, who were my two great, life mentors.

I never wanted my students to doubt that I was there for them and very happily so.

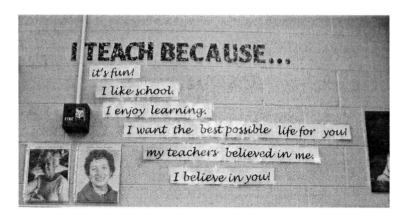

I Teach Because…I taught with these words in my classroom for over twenty years, reminding me of my life's calling.

Don't Burn Bridges

his may be more noticeable for me, because I have lived and worked in the same community for many years with it being the one in which I grew. I have never been one to burn bridges. I do know those people who will tell off people, stomp off in a huff, and generally leave a bad taste in someone's mouth and feel very satisfied that they have set that person straight or that they will never have to deal with that person again. But I have found that over the years we never know, especially when living in the same community for a long period of time, just how other people will weave and dovetail in and out of our lives and the significance they may have later, many years down the road.

I have been absolutely amazed how some seemingly casual meetings of long ago have blossomed into wonderful friendships, work experiences, or teaming. I would recommend to anyone: don't burn bridges. You may never know when you may want very dearly to walk across them. That's not to say you have to like or have high respect or esteem for everyone you meet. It is simply saying recognize everyone has good in them. Honor that good. And if your differences cause you to go different ways, go amicably. Don't burn bridges. You have no idea how those very same people may appear in your life many years in the future. It is always nice to meet a friend.

Drawing Birthday Cakes

*E*ver since the students' birthdays for the day began being announced in the mornings on the PA system at the end of the daily announcements, I had drawn each student I had a birthday cake for his or her birthday asking each what kind of cake was his or her favorite. I used quarter-sheet note pads from the supply room that were created from recycled, leftover information sheets, which had been glued together. I drew the cake with a lit candle (telling the student not to burn himself or herself) and printed, "Happy Birthday, *Student's Name*" on it. It was two-layered on a plate. I then added my signature smiley face with curly hair and signed my last name. If a student liked chocolate, I used a brown colored pencil to color the cake. If an ice cream cake were preferred, I drew one with ice cream cones. If he or she desired a carrot cake, I drew carrots. If marble cake were the choice, I drew marbles. You get the idea.

Once during my second hour prep period, I realized that I had missed making a cake for one of my first hour students as I had been busy readying materials for the day and lost sight of his birthday. When I determined this, I felt terrible. I immediately called the secretary and found out what class he had third hour. I zipped to the band room just prior to the classes changing and had his cake in hand waiting for him as I only needed to find out what kind he would like. This six-foot-plus, eighth-grade boy burst into a huge grin when he saw me with his cake. I apologized for not catching that it was his birthday earlier and asked what kind of cake he would like. He told me that chocolate was his favorite, and it just so happened that I had taken my brown colored pencil making it so he could have his favorite kind of cake. He was thrilled, and I was glad that I had corrected the omission.

This is not to say that I think every teacher should draw cakes for their students' birthdays. However, if a teacher can consistently do something that will be a perk to which their students look forward, lots of good will can be built.

Another time, one of my eighth-grade girls told me that her mother's birthday was Wednesday and asked me if I would draw a cake for her mother. Of course, I drew her mother a birthday cake. In fact, the mother had been one of my former students. The next day when I asked the daughter how her mother had liked her cake, she told me that she loved it and that it was hanging on their refrigerator!

Drawing birthday cakes for my students was a little thing that went a long way in good feelings.

Positive Points, Not Number Wrong

I used to mark wrong answers, total the number wrong on the page, total all pages of incorrect answers, and then covert the total wrong for the assignment to a positive number earned out of the points possible, placing that total on the front, also assigning a letter grade.

More recently, I marked wrong answers, totaled the number correct on each page and put it over the points possible for the page, and when done added all of the positive points together placing that total on the front over the points possible and attached the letter grade.

That represented a very subtle difference, but I do believe it sent the right message, emphasizing the ones that were correct from the get-go.

I could have gone one step farther and placed a "C" on each correct answer and marked nothing wrong only leaving those missed unmarked. I did not do that assuming there were many, many more right than wrong, and that would have been much more time-consuming. Admittedly, it would probably have sent a better message still.

Taking Grades Orally

After the first few years, I never took grades orally. I did for several years, but realized back in the mid-1980s that it was excruciating for some kids, cruel even. I always collected the papers and entered the grades. I thought it was important to afford them a safe environment as much as possible.

Using Red Ink

I long ago gave up using red ink on students' papers. It just seemed too glaring and obvious, as if it were screaming what was wrong rather than what was correct. It was a small thing, but they would never get any red ink from me. Amazingly, some noticed, commenting a few weeks into the school year that I didn't use red ink. Maybe I had my fill of red ink from my teachers. Who knows?

Comments on Students' Papers

I almost always put written comments on my students' papers in addition to the points scored out of the points possible and the letter grades. This became a useful tool for me. For perfect papers, I had five comments, and I put them on papers in the same order every time. So when I finished correcting the stack of papers for a particular hour, depending upon which comment I last used (and keeping track how many times I used the cycle of five), I knew exactly how many perfect papers there were.

My five comments, in order, for perfect papers were *Wowie-zowie, Razzle-dazzle, Super-duper, Yippy-skippy,* and *Yippy-zippy.*

For other A's and A-'s, I used one of the following in random order: *Great, Fantastic, Terrific, Fabulous, Fantabulous* (a self-made word), *Wowie, Hooray, Stupendous, Stellar, Snazzy, Spiffy, Awesome,* and *Excellent.*

For B+'s, I always used *Very Good.*

B's and B-'s received *Good.*

For C's, I used *Fine* or *Okay.*

D's earned *Hang in there, Focus, Keep working, Prepare carefully, Be sure to finish, Be sure to ask if you have questions, Think,* or *You're better than this.*

E's most often received *Better days ahead. I promise.* I have been later told that this was perceived as very enabling and motivating, encouraging them to try harder the next time.

My students often shared their comments with one another, and I think that simple act may have been one of the things many liked best about my class.

Folders

*F*or years and years, I gave my students manila folders the first day of class. The folders were to be distributed down the rows at the beginning of each class period and collected at the end. The students were to keep their work in them: on-going assignments, papers to have for future assignments, things to study, reading logs, and "whatever" pertaining to class.

I printed their last names on the tab using a different colored marker for each class. I also placed a colored line above the people's names who sat in the front of each row. It was the job of those to make sure their folders were on top of the pile for their row and that all of the folders were facing the same way with all tabs facing up when collected. That made disturbing the folders a no-brainer.

Their folders were to never leave the classroom.

I delivered ALL corrected assignments to their folders so as to not waste class time passing out papers. Also, if a student were absent, his or her folder remained on his or her desk during class. If I handed out anything, it was put in the absent student's folder. Upon the student's return, he or she had everything the others had received.

During the first marking period, I had been known to search folders for assignments not turned in to me as requested, still giving the students full credit if it were there. I told them the second marking period that I would no longer go "folder hunting."

I was also insistent that the folders be collected at the very end of the hour. A typical class could pass up folders in eight or nine seconds. If they passed them up too soon, I'd tell them they were suffering from PFP, Premature Folder Pass-up.

This was also cost-effective as most folders lasted the entire year.

After each test, I had them clean out their folders telling them what they should save, if anything.

For a few years long ago, I graded their folders before the tests to make sure they had saved the work they needed that I had specified to review for the test. I gave them three points for each designated piece they were to have saved making it an "easy A." I no longer did that in later years as I found it too cumbersome and time consuming. I still think it was a good idea in principle, just not in practice.

M-Squared Basket

For nearly my entire teaching career, I had a wire basket on my desk in which all of the students' papers were to be placed when due. Occasionally, I picked up their papers by having them pass them forward. But more often than not, they'd turn in their work as they finished it. I referred to the basket as the M-Squared Basket and labeled it such because it was made of **m**etal and held their **m**ental work – the Metal Mental Basket, or as it became fondly called, the M-Squared Basket. They always found that name to be very catchy. More importantly to me, they knew where to place their completed assignments.

During the first marking period, if assignments were not turned in to me when due, I would look in their classroom folders. After that, I no longer went hunting. Their completed work had to make its way to the proper spot – the M-Squared Basket.

Floor Cleaning

I made a big deal about the floor being cleared of trash, tiny paper bits, gum wrappers, candy pieces, or whatever. Of course, at the start of the day it was pristine, but after thirty-four first-hour kids or so, it was less so. While the next hour was being seated, I picked up the floor and when coming upon streamers from paper being torn from a spiral binder, I commented that someone must have had a celebration often re-scattering some of the picked up paper and hollering, *"Whee, science is FUN!"*

I told them that picking up the floor was my exercise program, and I stayed slim with all of the bending, so whoever was responsible for leaving the stuff on the floor was really "helping" me stay fit. Preposterous, of course, but they loved it, and more importantly, I believed they did "get the message" and were more careful about what they left on the floor in my classroom, the desired result.

Metacognition

*F*or many, many years, I asked my students, usually at the end of the first marking period, to think about what they thought of my class, i.e. metacognition, to think about what you're thinking. I had a series of questions about different aspects of the class and a space at the end of the two-sided document, so they could tell me anything else they wished. I found their responses interesting, and I respected their ideas. I can remember a comment made by a girl in eighth grade (I've since taught her nephew.) well over twenty-five years ago that changed the way I taught forever. She commented that when I wrote notes on the board and explained as I wrote that she could understand them better rather than having the notes on the board from the previous hour and my just talking about them in order. She said she tended to copy ahead and not listen as well to what I was explaining. Of course, back in that day, to avoid the cloud of chalk dust aggravating my contact lenses I did this. Since the day I read her comment, my notes were "fresh" for each hour whether in chalk, on the overhead, or from the data projector as in more recent years. With the data projector, I had the notes saved on my computer but only showed them as I spoke of the concepts.

I know her comment of long ago improved learning for many students over the years.

There have been other things said that also changed what I did, but that is the one comment that stood out as making a difference from the **very day** it was made and **every day** I taught after it.

Also, I always responded with brief comments in writing to many of their thoughts. It was a two-way street. Maybe something I said would change them for the better.

Additionally, those sheets were a real benefit, because I saved them for parent/teacher conferences that were held within a week of the first marking period ending. The kids were pretty honest, and the parents learned much about their child's thoughts about my class. I would send the sheet home with the parent(s) and ask them to discuss it with their child. For those whose parents didn't attend, I returned them to their folders so they could see my comments.

Delayed Paper Correcting

It is true and an absolute rule: the longer one waits to grade a set of papers, the longer it takes to grade them.

Haircuts and Such

$\mathcal{I}$ always found it so interesting how much the students noticed and their perceived entitlement to make comments. Whenever I got a haircut, I would invariably be asked, "Did you get your haircut?" To which I responded, "No, I have a knob on the back of my neck, and I rolled it in." They rolled their eyes, but they loved it.

Too, they always commented when I had colored my hair. Middle school was and still is a fascinating age with the students being involved, caring, and without pretense. They were simply interested and willing to freely ask, feeling connected to me, their teacher. I always tried to honor their questions and answer them honestly or factiously as in the haircut query.

Correct Grammar

*W*hen my students were telling me something and said, "Me and whoever," I would ask, "Who?" If the person didn't immediately catch on why I was asking, I would literally sound like an owl, repeating, "Who, who, who?" Still if the student didn't grasp the concept and why I was being so inane, someone would holler, "*The other's name* and I!" placing the nouns in the correct order. By the end of the year, few made that error in my presence. Cha-ching as it was a lesson learned and not even in language class.

Displaying My College Degrees

*O*ver twenty years ago while taking a seminar on effective teaching, it was recommended that we, as teachers, display our college degrees in our classrooms as they represented accomplishments of which we should be proud. Since that time while teaching, mine were proudly positioned in my classroom on a shelf for all to see. Many students would "read" them making positive comments.

Verb Verse

*W*hile teaching one day, something was said about language arts, and I told the class that I still remembered *The Verb Verse* from my seventh-grade language arts class in 1962-63. I was always and forever trying to get my students to speak correctly using proper (Is there any other kind?) grammar. *The Verb Verse* is a list of helping/auxiliary verbs, and saying it would help you to determine if a verb were one or not. Back in the day, this knowledge was essential in diagramming sentences. And yes, I still consider diagramming sentences an art form and essential to learning good grammar. When I saw the obituary of my seventh-grade language arts teacher who taught me *The Verb Verse* in the local paper one day, I quietly whispered, "Thank you."

The Verb Verse

Is, are, am, was, were, can, could,
Do, did, have, has, had, will, would
May, might, ought to, shall, must, should.

The Field Trip Smile

*L*ong ago when my friend and I taught summer school, we developed the "field trip smile." No matter what happened, we pasted on a smile and kept it throughout the day. No matter if it were kids throwing up, lost, in the road, hiding under the bus, an exaggeration but you get the idea, we maintained our field trip smiles. It has served me well over the years in many situations in school and beyond school. Whenever life becomes a little dicey, I revert to field-trip-smile mode, and calm seemingly prevails no matter what I am feeling inside, however uncertain.

My Miracle Ear

*F*or the last nineteen years of my career, I taught in the new wing. The science rooms were large with vaulted ceilings and were so acoustically designed, if you know anything about the parabolic microphone concept, that I could hear whatever was whispered at the back of the room from my desk some thirty-five feet from those whispering. My students would be working at the counters at the back and at the sides of the room, and I could hear whatever they whispered. It was simply the physics of the room, nothing particularly special about my hearing. I would join right in their conversations if they were trying to whisper, amazing many. I told them that I had a Miracle Ear. "Really?" they always asked.

"Why yes, how else do you think I can hear you?" was my standard reply. They were absolutely amazed that I had heard whatever, and it was undeniable as I responded with something appropriate to their conversations. Little did they know that if they would talk in normal tones as they discussed the assigned material, I couldn't particularly hear them especially what they were actually saying. It was the whispering that did them in, so to speak.

Every now and then, I would have students come to my desk and, while talking to me, quizzically peer at my ear. I'd tell them, "Oh, you can't see my Miracle Ear, as I have a special kind that is too small to be seen, and it's embedded deep in my ear canal," all the while looking very innocently at them. Many times when students have written about me or to me, one of their most often mentioned memories is my incredibly amazing hearing, never missing what they were whispering. I have taught students who graduated with my sons who still swear these many years later that I must have had a Miracle Ear.

Among my favorite memories are the times when one of my students would ask my younger son, "Does your mom have a Miracle Ear?"

He would always hesitate and then answer looking a little conspiratorial, "Well, she's told me to say no," adding to the mystique. The legend continues...

Mute Button

At the beginning of the school year in my students' folders (in which they kept their papers for the class as the folders stayed in the room, individual assignments could be taken home as homework, which was a novel concept to some), I gave each of my students a 4" x 4" piece of red construction paper. For my students, this became their personal Mute Buttons to stop me from incessantly repeating things.

The summer prior to beginning this practice, our local Rite Aid Pharmacy installed new picture printing equipment; the new machine came equipped with voice instructions. That feature so annoyed me, as it kept repeating what was to be done. As soon as possible, in the picture-printing process, I muted the voice instructions. One day while doing so, I had the thought that my students probably thought the same of my instructions, as I likely repeated them many times. Not wanting to be as annoying to them as the picture machine was to me, I decided to give each student a Mute Button. When flashed, I would stop (unless I was giving first-time instructions) my unnecessary repetition. They liked the power, and in most cases, I respected their wishes.

Band-Aids

*B*efore school in August, I would go to Walmart and buy a dozen or so boxes of Band-Aids, featuring various cartoon characters. These were for my students when they had a booboo. I kept them in my lower, right, desk drawer unannounced until someone needed a Band-Aid for which he or she would innocently ask. I would say that sure I had

Band-Aids, and that they were in my bottom, right, desk drawer and to help themselves. Upon opening the drawer, the student would squeal with delight no matter whether a boy or a girl. They all loved my Band-Aids. If the truth were to be known, I do believe some booboos were invented so the student could simply have one of my Band-Aids. Sure, the Band-Aids cost a few dollars, but very few when considering how much good will they built.

Kleenex

*T*he first day of school, I would tell my students that I would provide Kleenex (or Puffs, in any event a good kind of facial tissue that was dependably soft and fluffy) for them and that I personally purchased the boxes. I showed them the two areas of the classroom where they would be placed, by the phone and on my desk. I told them that they deserved the very best and to help themselves when needed. I bought a case of the rectangular boxes and a case of the square boxes. They lasted the entire school year. They were happy, and I was happy. This was one small courtesy suggesting I cared for them and their comfort.

Pencil Erasers

*B*efore school would start in the fall, I cruised the Walmart, Staples, Office Max, or Meijer's aisles looking for inexpensive arrow tip, pencil erasers. They were usually colorful and as many as forty for $1, so relatively inexpensive. I bought a bunch and had them available for my students. When they needed an eraser, I offered them one from my selection telling them, "My erasers are your erasers."

Did I think that we, as teachers, needed to purchase these things? No, but the good will built in doing so was priceless. The Kleenex, Band-Aids, and erasers all told my students that they were important to me. I am sure they had no idea that I paid for these things, but that was fine, too. I was the procurer and distributor, at the very least, and the items were for them.

Brownies

*I*n talking to my classes, it often came up that I was not the main cook in our house and only made about six things. Cooking wasn't something I particularly enjoyed, but I did like to prepare my few signature dishes for family and friends. Brownies were one of my specialties. Since brownies were fairly well liked by many, in celebration of my classes each marking period I made brownies for them, a very popular decision. It built immeasurable good will methinks.

Mondays: My High Days of Purpose

*W*hile teaching, I loved Mondays; I truly did. Before going to bed Sunday evening, in reality early Monday morning, I would have everything completed and ready for the week. When I awoke Monday, it was with enthusiasm and an agenda. I was all business, as Monday was my high day of purpose. I made my lists and busied myself accomplishing the items on them. On Mondays, I was a dynamo and didn't know the meaning of the word quit. I had a "can do" attitude and was filled with confidence and purpose. As the week continued, my efficiency and zest for tasks flagged a bit, and by Thursday, I was often in weekend mode.

In retirement, I still function much the same. If you want me to help in conquering the world, catch me on a Monday.

March Equals Malaise

*T*hese were my feelings in mid-March: we are here, mid-March. The best students are "forgetting" to turn in work. You spend an hour doing a fascinating lab, and they are clueless as to what was really happening or the intended learning. The lazy and lethargic have given up all pretense of work. The good students have parts of assignments missing. Oh yes, it's March!

One mid-March day, I told my principal, "Today, you could pull the shades and if I didn't look at what they were wearing, and some have been in flip-flops for a couple of months, after teaching one hour, I would know it is March." They were fidgety, flighty, giggly, way too social, and generally very pleasantly inattentive. And in truth, I was not too far behind them. Oh, how I welcomed spring break each year! Upon returning, whether it be in late March or April, the spell of March Malaise was broken. The students were engaged again, as was I.

Being Snarly

I found that near the end of winter, I tended to become snarly. I frustrated more easily, as I saw my students' potentials as so much more than they ever saw. I recognized that "time was running out" for me to have a positive impact on them and to enable them to catch a dream that would sustain them throughout their lives or be the springboard from which many more dreams would arise. Too, I am a being of light, and winters simply offered less daylight hours. This had an accumulating effect on my mood, causing a slow descent. In the later years, it was not as great of a downward spiral as in the earlier years, but nevertheless, I did tend toward impatience and had a harder time feeling the innate joy of living in those darker, winter days. With the coming of spring, the warmer weather, and longer daylight hours, I reaffirmed the perspective of all things being as they should be with Divine Order reigning.

At times, it was only when I began to emerge from the winter doldrums that I appreciated the spell that had been cast. I reawakened to life and again became thankful for a renewed spirit. It was then that I rose above being snarly.

Making Me Mad

*O*ne day, I was talking with a fellow teacher about those few students who seemed to have the unique ability to make us mad. It shouldn't have happened, but it occasionally did, at least for me. Over time, I have had a few students who could get under my skin with only a look. They represented the frustration I had in trying to teach the unwilling, the unwanted, and the not understood. Of course as an adult, I realized that in order for anyone to make me mad, I first must have given them permission to do so. But there were times with others to teach, things to do, papers to correct, plans to make, that it sometimes didn't take much to tip the sanity scales, and I gave them permission to make me mad. It seemed they were always the ones who didn't seem to care, often making me, the teacher, the only one in the equation who did. I was certainly not proud of those moments when I felt my anger growing. Hopefully, it was less than apparent to my students. We are all human; sometimes I forgot and allowed a student to "make me mad."

A Favorite Lesson Activity

$\mathcal{O}$ne of my favorite lesson activities was in teaching the skeletal system. To acquaint the students with the scientific names of the bones, I printed a sheet of thirty sticker labels for each class of thirty scientific names of the bones. I passed the sheet down the rows requiring each student to peel a label, state the name aloud, come forward, and stick the label on me at the appropriate bone site. I told them for the "more sensitive" ones that they could just point, and I would place it. Usually the sternum (breast bone) and coccyx (tailbone) were left to me to affix. Favorites were the mandible (lower jaw), maxilla (upper jaw), and cranium (skull) often resulting in the student rather proudly pressing the labels in their correct places on my head.

I had standard lines for certain bones and the general occasion: the cranium holds the brainium; I never met a carpal I didn't like; the teacher gave the student a sternum look; I'm all stuck up; and such.

Once the thirty bones had been correctly labeled, I then passed the empty label sheet down the rows asking each student to come forward, take a label, announce the common name and scientific name, and reaffix it to the sheet. This ensured that all labels were removed.

The activity took ten to fifteen minutes, made them chuckle, and created a memory of their science teacher being plastered with thirty labels, all for their learning. I was never successful in convincing my teaching partner to do this. Yes, it was an "up close and personal" lesson, but the students always respected me and seemed to genuinely enjoy the goofiness of sticking labels on me, their teacher.

A lesson plan executed and long remembered by students and teacher alike.

Call Me Anytime

$\mathcal{I}$n eighth-grade life science, the human body systems were normally taught at the end of the school year with the reproductive system being last. With the reproductive system, state-mandated, grade-appropriate AIDS information was also presented. Administration-approved movies like National Geographic's, *The Miracle of Life*, a clip of a C-section, a birthing film loop, and such were shown and discussed. For newer or less comfortable teachers, this unit was stressful.

I felt particularly well-suited for these lessons, having delivered our first son vaginally and having a Caesarian section for our second son. I told the students that anything could be asked, but using appropriate terms was required. If those were unknown, they could see me while work was being done by the others. I tried very hard to establish a relaxed, comfortable atmosphere.

To stress the significant growth of a fetus in the womb, I took in a pear and a watermelon. I turned the pear upside down and told my students that it represented the size of a normal uterus. On the other hand, the watermelon approximated the size of a full-term fetus ready to be delivered. Pear-watermelon: that's why it's called labor. Many said that they would never look at the produce section of the grocery store the same again.

Our school also had a policy of abstinence for its students. I emphasized the school's policy and told the students that it was fully endorsed by me. Furthermore, I told them that while a student of our school system, they could call me anytime, day or night as our phone in the bedroom was a foot or two from my head, if they found they were in a compromising situation. I would tell the person with them and them to wait and not have sex. "No, wait! Don't have sex!" was my mantra for them.

Yes, my phone rang at 2:30 a.m. one weekend with "the question." Over the muffled giggling, I recognized the caller's voice. Calling her by name, I told her not to have sex. Heightened giggling followed before the click of the receiver was heard. When returning to school, I learned the call was from a slumber party, and the caller was dared to make the call.

Another *anonymous* weekend call was received from a girl asking if she should have sex. "No, wait!" was emphatically stated by me just before she hung up the phone. In this case, our caller ID displayed her mother's name and number clearly. Monday before class began, I asked her if she took my advice. Mortified would best describe the look on her face.

The last call I received asking if the person should have sex was made about 9:30 p.m. one weekend by a male caller talking fast. He had stated his name but I missed it. When asked if I thought he should have sex, I asked if he were in school (meaning was he a student of our school). He said, "No," to which I replied, "Then you're on your own, because I have no right to tell you what to do if you're not in school." Monday after school, my younger son came home and asked why I had told *boy's name* that he was on his own, as he was a high school student. I noted that he said that he wasn't in school, to which he replied that no, the boy wasn't standing with a girl at his locker. Oops, missed that one!

Over the years, girls especially have told me with a grin that they still have my number if they need it. Of course, they were kidding, and I never expected to seriously be called. But in saying that, I do think they all knew, and still know, that I would be available for them in life if they ever needed me. Sometimes that's comforting to know.

Teaching Kids First

I was high school trained. I taught the subject. At the beginning of my career, the kids were quite secondary. I loved the subject.

I have always taught middle school, or junior high as it was called when I began my career. In the early years, I taught a high school class the last hour of the day and have taught applied math, biology, botany, zoology, and advanced biochemistry. Beginning in 1993, I taught elementary summer school for nine years. For those years, the grades taught ranged from second to sixth.

All to say, I have had a wide range of teaching experiences. Each age/grade had its charms and drawbacks. I found the high schoolers to be somewhat sedentary with a "teach me" attitude. They were very happy to sit back and have me do the work. The second-graders were Velcro children, always clinging to me. For me, my very favorite students to teach were seventh-graders from November through eighth-graders in late April. I told that to my seventh-graders one October, and I also told them that they would mature and "catch on" to things, to just give it some time and that by November they would be fine. They wanted to know what was "wrong" with them before November. I told them that they were too much like sixth-graders, racing through their assignments, not reading carefully, being only partially complete, and putting social issues ahead of class work. However, I assured them that by November they would have their priorities straight and be the best students they could be.

Someone ventured to ask what was "wrong" with eighth-graders after April. I quickly replied that their heads were in the high school, and they no longer wanted to do anything here.

My motto was, "Give me seventh-graders in November through eighth-graders in late April, and I am a happy camper. They are my faves."

Also, somewhere during my thirty-eight years, I transitioned to teach kids.

The profound change may have been initiated sometime during my nine-year stint of teaching summer school. There was not a shred of a doubt by the time that experience ended that I taught kids. The subject had become secondary.

I only wished that the evolution had been sooner in my career. I believe today that the best teachers teach kids first no matter the level.

The Friendly Student

A phenomenon I noticed for the past several years of teaching was that the students who seemed particularly friendly, outgoing, and interactive the first week of school (for which I am always thankful that I appear to be reaching at least some) often became as the year progressed far too friendly, talkative, and even mouthy. Their initial, welcomed bravado often wore thin as they became more comfortable. By Christmas, I was usually wishing they would be quiet, not share their every thought, and just sit in their seats once in a while.

Feeling Safe

*A*s much as possible, I tried to create a "safe" atmosphere in my classroom. Beyond the obvious physical safety, I very consciously extended that to emotional safety. I would hope that my students knew that they would not be publicly belittled for their choices or omissions. Yes, I did publicly ask them for late work, but tried to respect them as people. If heard, I curbed any other attempts by others to ridicule, harass, or defame them. I wanted them to know my room was a *safe* place to be.

Seeing Your Students in Different Settings

*H*aving returned from a band concert, I had the thought that it was always interesting to see your students in different settings. Some became outgoing and confident; some seemed shyer, and others displayed talents not expressed in the classroom. It was helpful to see them in other settings and reminded me that "my world" wasn't the only place one may function and succeed.

Also, I had taught over half of the parents of my current students in later years. It was always very interesting to see them as parents, grown, mature, and ably living their lives, which absolutely warmed my heart.

Separating the Student from His or Her Work

T had to keep reminding myself that the student was different from his or her work. The person was a wealth of possibilities, ever changing with hope shining brightly. His or her work may not have reflected such optimism. The person was ever worthy; the quality of the work at times may not have been worth much of anything. Change was always possible. As long as there was life, there was hope.

I had an aide somewhat whimsically comment once that some of my students had never received a behavior reward sheet and never would. That was a fundamental difference between the two of us. She truly thought some never would earn one. I thought all would possibly one day earn one. The problem was that I may not have had them as students long enough to see that worthy moment, but I believed it existed and was possible.

Getting Them Through

The longer I taught middle school, the more I came to believe that we, as their teachers, were not so much about teaching them the subject material, but rather just getting them through adolescence whole, complete, intact, with the most positive self-image possible. Over the years, I evolved in the way I saw my job. In later years, I began seeing my job as finding their strengths, building upon them, accommodating for their weaknesses, making them stronger, and giving them the belief in themselves that would carry them with confidence to be lifelong learners, able to confidently pursue their dreams.

My Hardest Job as a Teacher

*B*esides counting the number of papers correctly to pass down a row, the most difficult job I had as a teacher was convincing my students that they were, indeed, capable of great things. I knew this about them, but many of them did not accept this as true. With vision, a dream, work, and focus, they could truly become whatever it was in life that they desired. Believing that was a possibility, and converting it to a reality was fundamentally in their hands.

We, as teachers, could be the spark and often nudged, pushed, and shoved them to reach beyond their present selves and believe in their futures. As Eleanor Roosevelt has said, "The future belongs to those who believe in the beauty of their dreams." I felt a teacher's job was to help his or her students foster and nurture beautiful dreams.

Teaching After Having a Child

*W*hen I returned to teaching, after having our first son, a friend asked me if it were really hard to leave my baby and return to work. I said that I knew he was well and with someone who actually knew what she was doing, so that was a relief in case inept me didn't notice something ominous. But I went on to tell her that I now understood how important each child I taught was in the eyes of his or her parents: someone so precious and incredible like none other. That was reason enough for me, a teacher, to return to school and give it my very best each and every time I stepped into my classroom. Parents entrusted me with their children, the very best children they had. It was for me to respect and honor that trust, being the very best teacher I could possibly be.

Being a Parent and Teaching

*A*s I saw younger teachers raising their children and teaching daily, I admired them, wondering how they could do it all. In reality, I knew because I had. Teaching while being a parent took tremendous planning and balancing. My hat is still off to all who do. I better understand, today being retired with my two sons grown, what it took than I did while doing it. To those of you teaching and raising a family whether you are a mother or father, I would say be gentle with yourself and know you are incredibly awesome!

Also, I would suggest that you try to leave the day's problems at school. I know there were times after being ever understanding and nice to errant students all day that I became "monster mother" in the van on the ride home. If one of my sons even hinted at a small infraction during his school day, I was all over him about it. In reality, the people who deserved my wrath but were spared in the name of professionalism probably never guessed my extreme frustration. Looking back, I know I had no business being so unrelenting with my sons on those occasions and that I was only transferring my frustration to them. As a parent who was a teacher, I would recommend trying to avoid this, although, in part, it comes with the territory.

When our older son turned sixteen, he drove to school and took his younger brother home after school. After my school day, I began going to a fitness center, complete with a pool. Sometime later, I became its Saturday water aerobics instructor for several years. Those early days of going to the gym and/or pool after school elicited this response from my younger son, "You sure are in a lot better mood when you come home from the club than you are right after school." Enough said.

A Two-Way Street

I always tried to remember that we, as teachers, weren't just the givers in the teacher-student relationship. Many times over the years, I have received encouragement from my students. I remember particularly tight financial times on the farm and not knowing if we'd "make it" or not. An especially difficult time was when an arsonist burned two of our barns. The money was tight and the stress was high. I was glad to go to school and be completely absorbed in being a teacher, leaving home cares behind for awhile. I welcomed being at school with the kids doing something positive and getting away from the constant worry, if only for a bit. The students' welcoming smiles at my door always cheered me.

During my last year teaching, one day when I was going to my room first thing in the morning, lost in thought, a sixth-grade girl touched my shoulder, smiled, and said, "Have a nice day." I needed that.

School was definitely a two-way street, as I received so much from my students in the way of purpose and the lessening of other life worries. I am ever grateful to them.

Closed-Mouthed

I always and truly appreciated any administration's closed-mouthed, respectful handling of discipline regarding students. It was also a confidentiality issue of importance; over the years, I have seen issues handled in a variety of ways. On some occasions, when a student had committed an error of discretion, it was spread like wildfire by all of the employees, administration, and staff alike. With a raised consciousness of confidentiality in later years, upon a grievous offense being committed, only those immediately involved were made aware of the situation. I thought that was good. Moreover, it was the high road. We, as a staff, were made aware of situations on a need-to-know basis. When an issue truly did involve the entire staff, prompt notification was made whether by an announcement (often coded), an e-mail, or a designated gathering. A five-minute stand up teachers' meeting explaining a homemade bomb rumor was an example of the latter.

Favorite Quote for My Students

$\mathcal{O}$ne of my very favorite quotes in life and for my students is from Eleanor Roosevelt, *"The future belongs to those who believe in the beauty of their dreams."*

I gave this to my students often, having them copy it in their science notebooks at the beginning of the year, telling it to them here and there as the year progressed, and at the beginning of the last marking period I would include it in a written statement that I gave them to encourage them to do their very best and not let up near the end of the year. It has served me well. I always felt that it was my job as a teacher to encourage them to have beautiful dreams and to help put foundations under those dreams, making them realities.

Maya Angelou

I was privileged to see Maya Angelou in person several years ago. She talked about the stage although seemingly empty except for herself being filled with those who had helped her get where she was in life. She stated that she was never alone but supported by all those who had helped her. She was grateful for each one.

When we stop to think of it, we all have our "stages" filled with those who have given to us and helped us become the people we are. Let's spend at least a few moments appreciating them.

Nancy Reagan

I heard Nancy Reagan say once that children are not a report card on their parents. I suppose as teachers, we often assumed any behavioral abnormalities were parent-generated. I certainly thought so before becoming a parent. Although I still believe parents are vital to their child's development, I will concede that each child has a mind of his or her own, a unique will and agenda. Sometimes these were at cross purposes to their parents' wishes for them. We, as teachers, needed to address the child's deficiencies and not worry so much about their causes; however, having said that, we, as teachers, also greatly benefited from having the parents' support in whatever we were doing educationally, if we were to ultimately succeed on a regular basis.

Assessment Goals: A Moving Target

$\mathcal{O}$ne of the most certain things about public education is that what is in vogue today is gone tomorrow, only to most likely reappear again with a new name, reinvented, and revived. As a new teacher, I was appalled at the casual attitude with which my department treated the Mager objectives in the early '70s. Yes, we had to, must even, align every lesson we taught to Mager's objective format. I was hustling to align my lessons and seemingly the only one sensing any urgency. One senior member of the committee said that the text book companies would soon have objectives for each lesson taught, so we could use those once created. Others took a "wait and see" attitude. I was new and ready to do whatever I was told *now*. Hindsight proved my colleagues wiser than I as soon we were on to something else.

About twenty years ago, portfolios became the rage. Every student had to have a portfolio that would follow him or her throughout school. We spent time creating entries, teaching to them, and earnestly making samples. The child's portfolio was to be the most significant piece of one's education. Upon retiring, I hadn't heard the word portfolio even mentioned in regard to students in the last five years.

A few years ago we were aligning our curriculum to Benchmarks, Standards, and Strands. Then entered the GLCE's and HSCE's, which have recently morphed to another form of assessment with yet others lurking just around the ever elusive corner. And if like the rest, they will surface, create work, require experts, and then fade, evolving into something else.

At times, education seems much like a well constructed PowerPoint presentation with one great idea seamlessly blending into another and then another and yet another, endlessly. It may sound cynical, but I think largely we are trying to hit a moving target and guess what is or isn't important within our discipline deemed by those at the state level who may or may not be on the cutting edge of the topic. What the proponents of the new and better ideas do have is the State Department of Education's ear, so we must comply with the mandates to the extent able before the newer, better horizon appears. In spite of all of this, students learn.

Special Education

$\mathcal{O}$ ver my years in education as a student and a teacher, my views of the special education student have changed.

When a student, those students in special education seemed more challenged than those I saw more recently. This could be because I was in the accelerated section and on the fast track in virtually all of my classes, starting in junior high and continuing through high school. By the time we were in high school, our college bound futures dictated a different path from those in special education. Maybe that created the perceptual difference that I remembered.

Whenever completing a round of IEP's to schedule special education students for their high school classes, I truly appreciated the abilities and strengths of our special education students. I had several mainstreamed in my classes and found them to be conscientious, industrious, friendly, pleasant, and by and large doing the very best they could. I respected and honored their abilities, remembering that they were still kids with frustrations, problems (real or imagined if only by them), and varied interests. I saw them more as people in need of "a special leg up" regarding some aspect of their education. Once the intervention was accomplished, I witnessed them blending very nicely with the general population with its myriad of differences, strengths, and weaknesses.

Special education in my view served the students well doing just what it was supposed to do for its clients, targeting difficult areas and providing skills and time for them to be mastered. I remain, even in retirement, an ardent supporter of special education.

My Final Thoughts to Them

I honored each student. The last day or so of class, I gave them a quarter sheet of brightly colored card stock with this final handout containing my exiting message for them. On the lines, I listed at least three or four things that I especially appreciated about them as a student. I am sure many, possibly most, were subsequently tossed with little thought. But for a few, I know it was important. For those, it was always worth the effort. Following is a sample.

June 2010

<u>*Student's Name*</u>,

Please know; it has been my pleasure to have been your science teacher (*or whatever class*) this year. I will look back on this year with fondness. I have especially appreciated you for...

_____

_____

_____

_____

_____

_____

_____

Best wishes in your future,

Michele Hile

Works-in-Progress

*W*e are all works-in-progress, and a teacher is no different. Please, don't think I had the "end all" of insight. Really, I had just some ideas that worked for me. Also, don't think that I employed what I knew the best skills to be all of the time either. I would get behind, pressed, and anxious. When in such states, probably more often than I cared to admit, I was most certainly not modeling what I knew to be teaching's best. I snapped at them sometimes and later hoped they were resilient enough to snap back. I was human, trying my best. Knowing the goal did keep me closer to the mark. In remembering my humanity, it was easier to accept and celebrate the students' humanity.

Earned Credentials

*T*here is no substitute for becoming a better teacher than teaching. Trying things and determining what works for you is the essence of great teaching. What works for one will not necessarily work for another and vice versa. And not everything will work every time. All to say, one must be in the classroom teaching to find one's way. Becoming an expert teacher really is something that has to be acquired through doing. Teaching day in and day out, year in and year out, will give a person understanding and perspective that can be earned no other way. To truly understand what we as teachers do, you must have done it, too. There exists no shortcut.

Where the Magic Happens

For those of us who were fortunate enough to have our own classroom, which was not the case in all schools, we needed to make it our own, reflecting our unique personalities. It needed to be pleasing to us, as we were the ones who would be spending a good part of our lives there. It should have been made inviting and friendly, upbeat even. When I taught in Kern Hall, the bulletin boards at the back of the room always looked better than the ones at the front probably because it was those that I saw. A classroom is very literally the place in which some students will catch the spark of their lives' dreams. It *is* where the magic happens. Make sure it is a place in which you can thrive.

No Place Else I'd Rather Be

*D*uring my introductory statement to each class in the fall, I told the students a bit about myself. I listed things like I was living in the house in which I grew up so I had all of my own old junk. I mentioned that I was a Caro High School graduate who never expected to teach in my home town. When I began my search, jobs were scarce and being offered a position in Caro, I took it thinking that I would be here two years tops. What I found was my life.

I had always thought that those who went to college would meet someone there who would become their spouse and live in a suburb of Chicago or some other large city. Not that I thought there was anything wrong or negative about returning to Caro, I just didn't expect it to happen to me.

On the first day of class, I would tell my students of the places I had been, having traveled extensively in my earlier days. I told them that I had kissed the Blarney Stone so that was why I talked all of the time. I mentioned having crossed the International Date Line and having had two Friday the thirteenths in a row, making me basically weird. I told them that their parents had probably told them not to talk to strangers and there was no one stranger than I, but I assured them that I was safe. I also told them that I had taught many of their parents and that meant that I was old. But I assured them that I would be old anyway and that I was much happier being old and having had their parents than not.

I concluded this litany by telling them that if my family members were well, there was absolutely no place else that I would rather be than in my classroom, teaching them at that place and time. I stood by that statement my entire thirty-eight-year teaching career.

Odds
and
Ends

My Mission Statement as a Teacher

$\mathscr{T}$his recaps topics in other entries but I thought it worth sharing.

To Be a Teacher – Mission Statement
Michele Hile
August 17, 2008

As I am beginning my thirty-seventh year of teaching middle school, my mission statement of what it means to be a teacher has changed dramatically. Trained as a secondary, subject-oriented teacher, I held knowledge to be the all-powerful driving force of my every plan. I taught science, period. Like me or not, I thought it of no consequence. Learning the material was the sole essential.

Now, I teach students, liking them and hoping they like me at least enough to "buy into" the program. Today, for me, to be a teacher means being a positive role model, encouraging, and enabling students to reach their maximum potentials. This has little to do with the subject taught, but everything to do with the persons they are to become. I want them to experience success and set goals that will lead them to a future full of promise. I am now a cheerleader shouting, "Yes, you can!" when the world is telling them otherwise. I am there for them, to always believe in their possibilities, an encourager of hard work, specific goals, and attaining their dreams. As Eleanor Roosevelt has said, "The future belongs to those who believe in the beauty of their dreams." When they no longer believe in their dreams, I do, and I hold up a mirror before them until they recapture the vision of their dreams. My motto is, "If there's life, there is hope." As Flavia Weeden has written, "'What is as important as knowledge?' asked the mind. 'Caring,' answered the heart." Today, I teach students, and I will care forever.

Teaching Partners

$\mathscr{I}$ have had two marvelous teaching partners. My first four years were spent with Suzanne Kirk, a woman three years older than I, who was raised in a neighboring community. I had known her from my 4-H horse days, and also her father was a competing farmer selling a different brand of seed corn than my father. You always knew your competition. Our family had long liked and respected hers. Many a Monday morning, she would be coming out of her room as I was coming out of mine on my way to hers. The question was always the same, "What are you doing today?" Many plans were hastily made in the hallway until I grew my sea legs, and we could actually plan after school or during our prep periods when we had them the same hour. We loved bouncing ideas off of one another. We became fast friends, planning our lessons together, discussing discipline, and sharing lunches.

When she left to live in another state, she recommended a replacement for her position, a woman who had worked as a permanent sub in our school system. Many other positive factors would come into play, and with my enthusiastic endorsement, she was hired.

My second partner, Barb Ruckle, and I taught together for thirty-four years. Not only did we become teaching partners, we also became best friends in life, raising our collective five sons together and living on adjoining pieces of farm land. As I am typing this, I look north to her home a quarter of a mile from ours, just down the road in farm country. I often notice her get her mail, play with her dogs, and mow her lawn. It is very comforting having her as a friend and neighbor. We worked together so well that I could stand at the back of her room in the doorway that led to our science prep room to which I had a door, and just stand there looking at her. She would always answer the question I hadn't yet asked.

What a wonderful experience it was to be so in tune to one another! Too, the things I particularly enjoyed doing, with respect to lesson preparations, weren't her favorites. Conversely, her favorites weren't mine. So for thirty-four years we worked, magically combining the very best of both of us to present a united package for our students. She has also been the principle encourager of this book. Many thanks, Barb!

My older son always said, with respect to my retiring, that Barb and I should teach a combined one hundred years. Well,

My teaching partners. On the left is Suzanne Kirk, and on the right, Barb Ruckle. Together we collaborated and offered a quality science curriculum.

we didn't make it quite that far. When I retired, I had taught thirty-eight years, and at that time Barb had just finished her thirty-fourth year. We did make a combined seventy-two years. I know John feels we fell short. I am thankful for the time we had together.

It was a joy and a privilege to work with these two dedicated women, excellent teachers both.

The Wonderful People

I certainly have met wonderful people in education. Once in a while, I will go somewhere and hear people talking about the lazy teachers. "What do you think about the lazy teachers?" they will ask me. Quite honestly, I don't know any. All I know are dedicated people who every day are doing their very best for the students of our community. If someone tends to be lazy, education is not the place for him or her; they simply do not stay. For six or seven hours or class periods a day, teachers are "on" front and center or guiding at the side, controlling, supervising young lives, encouraging, and giving legs to their students' dreams. It has been my privilege to work with the people I have. They were absolutely wonderful. Is that to say they were all alike? No, each had different strengths; each had fortés; each had different things to offer to his or her students. But all were wonderful in their own way. It has been my privilege to have served for thirty-eight years as a public school teacher and work with such supremely dedicated and grand people. I stand by that.

*Lynn (Orlowski) Jensen, Barb Ruckle, Sarah (Ransford) Baird,
and I, still enjoying our time together and learning from one
another. Lynn and Sarah were my students in the early 1980s.*

Twenty-One-Year Cycle

For whatever reasons, significant people seem to pop up in my life in twenty-one-year periods. Gladys Wiltse, my huge life mentor, was forty-two years older than I. Suzanne Harwick, my tenth-grade biology teacher and life mentor, is twenty-one years older than I. Sarah and Lynn were students of mine and became babysitters for Barb (my dear friend, neighbor, and teaching partner of thirty-four years) and me. They are twenty-one years younger than I. We have remained close, and I attended their weddings and can tell you their children's birthdays, celebrating each one. I often wonder, "Who is in the world forty-two years younger than I with whom I will have a significant relationship?" And just think, soon another "connection" for me to find will be born. Life is amazingly interesting methinks.

Room Numbers Plaque

I proudly have displayed in our sunroom a plaque with the following room number plates: 102, 109, 103, and 101. These were the actual room number plates once affixed above the doorways of rooms in Kern Hall, the first portion of the Caro High School complex built on Hooper Street in 1957. The plaque represents more than forty years of my life. Each room holds special significance for me.

Room 102 was my ninth-grade civics classroom with Mrs. Wiltse (Gladys Garner Wiltse to be precise) being the teacher. As mentioned previously, Gladys became my life mentor. She had a message I needed hearing during a particularly difficult and awkward time of my life. I was identifying with my father's infidelity and in some twisted way felt responsible for his choices.

Although long-divorced from my mother, I had just learned that his summer vacations "with a fellow from work" had been taken for a few years with a married woman. The realization of my father's vacationing partner was crushing to a fourteen-year-old. I felt as though I had a sign on my forehead stating, "My father is dating a married woman!" I felt worthless.

Gladys had the message that no matter what situation you came from, at this age, you were responsible for you. You were in charge of your life and could make it anything you desired. Careful planning and hard work could be your ticket to anything you wanted including feeling honorable and not burdened by a father's indiscretions. The message took, and I am still striving daily to be the person Gladys Wiltse showed me I could be.

Gladys's last year teaching was my first. The following summer, I accompanied her and her husband as her fifteen-year-old granddaughter's roommate on a twenty-six-day trip around the world visiting Greece, Egypt, Lebanon, India, Iran, Thailand, fueling in South Vietnam, Hong Kong, Taiwan, Japan, and Alaska. During that trip, I experienced two Friday the thirteenths in a row, having one in Japan and again the next day in Alaska. I always told my students that experience was what made me weird.

The following summer, I went on a trip to the British Isles with Gladys and her husband along with a few others. Many an hour I have sat at Gladys's kitchen table by the bowed window discussing life. In February of 2003, I was honored to deliver her eulogy. What began in Room 102 has remained with me. For many years, her photo hung in my classroom by a saying that in part read, "My teachers believed in me." I also taught language arts in Room 102 one hour several years ago while my regular room was being used by a science class.

Room 109 was significant, because that is where I had tenth-grade biology with Suzanne Harwick. It was her first year teaching in Caro, returning to the classroom having two children a few years younger than I at home. She taught seventh-grade reading and spelling and one high school biology class. I fell in love with the subject and admired the teacher. When I became a senior, I was a cadet in one of her reading and spelling classes. She let me plan and deliver lessons occasionally under her close supervision. That was the best training I could have had in becoming a teacher. I earned my bachelor's degree, majoring in biology. I taught with her as a colleague for eleven years before she retired. Her picture also hung in my classroom. Last August, I had a delightful lunch with her in Charlevoix, Michigan, where she spends her summers when not at her winter home in Florida.

Room 103 was important because it was the first room in which I taught, being there two years, and the room in which I had eighth-grade science foreshadowing my thirty-eight-year teaching career, which was mostly eighth-grade science.

By the estimation of most, and me included, **Room 101** was the best room in Kern Hall. It had a brick back wall, not cement blocks, and I knew everything that happened in the hall as all had to pass by on their way to and from the office. It was the happening place. It was in Room 101 that I took on the persona of the "mother" of sorts of the middle school. In addition to it being my eighth-grade math and history room when I was a student, I taught in Room 101 for seventeen years.

Together as a student or a teacher, I have spent a combined twenty-three very happy and meaningful years in those rooms. The plaque reminds me daily from where I have come.

The List

$\mathcal{S}$tarting about my fourth or fifth year of teaching, I began keeping a list of those students who had died that I had taught. I "caught up" the former years and then added names as I learned of a student's passing. Morbid you might say; honoring their lives I would prefer to think.

The list included the student's name, age, date of death, and cause. I purposely carried this list with me in my purse until I retired having to add little rectangles of paper as the years progressed. Too, I recognized that there were those whom I had taught that had moved away and died of whom I had no knowledge. Over that, I had no control.

When I retired, I removed the list from my purse and wondered if I would continue to keep track. During that summer shortly after retiring, I officiated the funeral of a young man I had taught. I had grown up with his family being our friends and neighbors.

I came home from his funeral and entered his name on the list, knowing as I wrote that it would be the last name I recorded. It wasn't that I no longer cared; it was becoming overwhelming, and the list would only increase. His name was number eighty; yes, eighty of my former students I knew to be dead. Also, there had to be others.

For the most part, my students per class numbers were fairly low in my final years of teaching with many classes having from twenty to twenty-five students. I would look at my classroom on any given day and think that three or possibly four classrooms of students whom I had taught were no longer living. That thought never failed to sober and amaze me. In particular, it reminded me to do my level best each and every day each and every hour that I taught.

I honor each student I have taught, living or dead.

Small Pencil Collection

In the early 1990s, an eighth-grade boy stood at my desk and showed me a really short pencil. He said, "Don't you just love short pencils?" with a big smile. I told him that I had never really thought about it before, but yes the pencil was, indeed, "cute." He then said, "Here, do you want it?" to which I replied, "Sure," and took the pencil placing it in my desk drawer, giving it little more thought. A few days later, he offered me another short pencil. Then, I began noticing short pencils and picking them up off of the floor and saving them. Over time, other students noticed my interest and offered me their short pencils. I even believe some students "created" short pencils to give to me.

I continued this tradition began by that friendly, insightful student long ago, and had nearly 1,000 short pencils by my

My small pencil collection began when a student gifted me his small pencil.

retirement. I kept them in clear, plastic, gallon containers in my home office. Each May, I took them to school and showed my students, telling them about the collection's genesis. I did supervise them very carefully not wanting to lose any of my interestingly collected pencils.

Two summers ago, I was asked to be the Teacher Speaker at the combined Caro High School Class Reunion of the Classes of 1978 and 1979. The boy's mother talked to me that night. She was a former student of mine, as was his dad, and his aunt and uncle, too. I told her about my small pencil collection that was begun by her son and how it had grown over the years. She told me that he was in the Armed Services protecting our freedom. I took a picture of me and my pencils, wrote a note to him, and sent it to her so she could forward it to him.

I contemplated all of the things the pencils "have seen" and the stories they could have told. All the while, I smiled and thought of the long-ago day when an eighth-grade boy gave me a really short pencil.

A Teacher's Funeral

*I*n my final year of teaching, I officiated the funeral of a family friend with whom I had exchanged birthday cards, Christmas cards, and letters for over forty years. She was a retired third-grade teacher from a neighboring district having taught thirty-nine years. As part of the service, a former student of hers, who became a very accomplished woman and active community member, was asked by the deceased's daughter to read a letter that she had written to her mother on the occasion of her mother's eightieth birthday ten years earlier. This woman read her letter with passion and love. I think sometimes we as teachers have no idea the positive and long-lasting difference we make in people's lives.

My Intensive Care Nurse

*I*n February of my thirty-seventh year of teaching, I became very ill. I had pneumonia with three other infections, hospitalizing me in the critical care ward for a week. What I remember is that I was just so very tired; I didn't hurt but could barely navigate. That particular Friday, it took me over ten minutes sitting on the edge of our bed just to put on my shoes and socks. I recognized that as very telling. I had my husband take me to the emergency care center, and from there I was transported to the main hospital for admittance. I can easily say that was the sickest I had ever been, possibly not feeling the sickest, but I was told that if I had not sought help but had decided to stay home and just go to bed that I very possibly would have never awakened. A similar event had happened to the aunt of one of my first hour students earlier that school year, so I could appreciate what my medical care team told me, knowing my condition was critical. My ketone levels were through the roof endangering my very life. From the various infections, I became a Type 1 diabetic and remain so. Happily, the condition is managed very well today, and I feel wonderful.

In truth, I am probably healthier than I have ever been in my entire life sans having a chronic, serious condition.

Back on that February Friday as I was settling into my intensive care room, which pretty much just required me to lift my eyelids and recognize that I was indeed in a hospital room, a nurse came breezing into the room. She cheerfully said, "Hi, I'm (Name), your ICU nurse for the night." She briskly walked across the room to the computer near the window to the right of the foot of my bed. On that, the sickest day of my life with the nurse swiftly entering the room, turning to greet me, and standing in front of the computer accessing my information, a brain cell or two of mine must have been working. I looked at her and almost inaudibly whispered with a rasping voice and great effort, "Where did you go to school?" There was just something about looking at her from the side and hearing her voice that seemed very familiar, sparking recognition. She was probably in her early forties.

"What's that?" she asked.

"Where did you go to school?" I repeated with great effort.

"Oh, I grew up in a little town about thirty miles east of here, Caro," she innocently offered.

Mustering all of my energy, I said, "I think I was your eighth-grade science teacher."

She spun around and looked me directly in the face and gasped, "Oh, my gosh, Mrs. Hile, it's you!" Yes, indeed, it was, whatever was left of me.

Not only had I taught her, but her niece was one of my students that very year.

On the sickest day of my life, a woman who I had probably not seen in twenty-five or thirty years re-entered my life, and

I recognized her as one of "my girls." From that moment, I knew everything would be all right. I was in good hands.

Connections

$\mathcal{I}$ never cease to marvel at how circumstances keep bringing back former students into my life in many and varied ways. On our thirty-fifth anniversary, my husband and I went to Bennigan's for dinner before attending a Jim Brickman concert. The restaurant and concert venue were thirty miles from our home town in a much larger city. As the hostess was seating us, we were told the name of the girl who would be our waitress. I immediately thought, "I wonder?" Yes, the girl was a former student of mine, as were her father, her mother, her aunt, her uncle, and her cousin. She and I were genuinely glad to see one another. When she brought our meals, she told me that another Caro student said to say, "Hi," and to be sure to tell Mrs. Hile that he cooked the meal. In addition, he said to tell me, "Academic Track Boys' Quartet!" He had not been a student of mine, but he was in the Boys' Quartet of Academic Track for which another teacher friend and I were coordinators for many years. After our meal, we were brought a huge, delicious, raspberry cookie and ice cream dessert for our anniversary with the compliments of our waitress, the chef, and another girl who was the waitress in another section of the restaurant and had been a former student of mine as well.

If that weren't enough, I had thought during dinner that the woman at the table behind us looked familiar. I was at the point in my life that most people looked a bit familiar, so I didn't think too much about it. When her husband stood to put on his coat (he was seated behind my husband, so I couldn't see him during dinner), I realized it was a man and woman both of whom I had taught along with most of their brothers and sisters and one of their two children. What a night! I probably saw more people I knew while dining in the city thirty miles from our home than I would have known in a home-town restaurant.

I always welcome former students into my life and am thankful for having taught them. Happily, many reciprocate.

More Connections

As I settle into my retirement years busying myself with other things, mostly non-school related, I am ever appreciative of those former students I see while out and about in public. Many times, they recognize me first. They often call me by name, or if I had them early in my career, they may ask if I were a teacher to begin the conversation. It seems my former students are everywhere, at least in my home town. Without fail, every trip to town or casual errand involves contact with someone I've taught even if it's simply seeing someone on the street. I love running into them and the quick reminiscing, always continuing on my way with a happy heart.

The student connections continue to amaze me even after leaving teaching. I am grateful for each one.

Keys

*I*t was always a special feeling to come into the school building on weekends, week nights, or other times that no one else was there and let myself into the building. It reminded me of how privileged I was to be working at our school as a teacher. The very air seemed to tell me I was where I belonged.

Innovations

*A*s technology became increasingly part of our day-to-day lives, it was easy to forget from whence we had come. My "trip" had been longer than most reading this account.

Overhead projectors were common in the mid-sixties and used daily in our math classes. I began college in the fall of 1968 and felt state-of-the-art with an electric typewriter as my sole convenience beyond paper, pens, and pencils. Being electric, it was considered a huge advancement over the manual typewriters, which were the norm of the day. When I began teaching in the fall of 1972, we had a mimeograph machine that used aromatic, blue ink we all, as students, liked to inhale when the copies were "fresh." That fact might explain a lot about our generation.

A few years later, we had a machine that could make overhead transparencies using a heat process. I can clearly remember when the salesman delivered to our office in Kern Hall our building's first Canon copier, an actual photocopier to be precise. I believe it was 1980 or at least close to that date. When I ended my career, we were a far cry from the overhead (although still in use for some applications), the mimeograph machine, and the transparency maker of former days. In my later years, our world routinely included a phone and TV in each classroom, white boards, data projectors, computers connected to the Internet or at least the part that was not blocked, and Elmos. Beam me up, Scotty!

Book Club Discussion on Education

One night at book club, we were talking about our parents and grandparents and their values of education. I mentioned that my maternal grandparents saw absolutely no need for my mother to continue her education beyond eighth grade. That made me think of them as very small, but in truth they were wonderful people in my eyes with that being a bit of a dichotomy for me still. One of my friends suggested that in the time they lived, the Great Depression era, they were probably thinking that they were doing the right thing by my mother, protecting her even. It was a different time and a different day.

Another friend mentioned that her grandfather always said that when you educated a man, you educated one person. But when you educated a woman, you educated an entire family. He saw a woman's education as much more important and far reaching. I found that perspective interesting.

Time of Day Writing

*T*his is something interesting that I noticed several years ago. I write a lot of cards, and yes, I use snail mail, because there is something very kinesthetic about holding a card and rereading the words and looking at the handwriting on the page. As my hands have more arthritis than earlier days, I don't hand write as much as I used to, especially if I have several things to say. Typing is so much faster and easier for my hands. But there is something very personal and very comforting about a hand-held card, at least for me. I have found what I write in the daytime to early evening, I write from my head. Hopefully, it is well written, but the thoughts are very controlled, very acceptable, and very intellectual.

Conversely, I have found when I write later at night (My time to shine is from 10:00 p.m. to 3:00 a.m.), I write from my heart. I am much more willing to say that I am thinking about the person with love or that he or she is prayerfully in my heart. Writing things from my heart makes the message much more meaningful.

I can literally read what I have written and tell what time of day it was composed, early in the day or late at night, not necessarily to the hour. I can determine if it were written from the intellectual, head perspective or from the emotional, heart perspective. When I write cards of comfort to people who are ill or who are going through a challenging life event, I really try to write late at night to ensure I will be writing from my heart. I believe the recipient deserves my best, and that is always from my heart.

The Understanding Child

*E*very now and then, a child came along with uncommon understanding of the world. Maybe it was not such an uncommon understanding as it was an understanding that meshed with my own. Glances were exchanged; understandings were recognized. Two souls were aligned. It didn't happen often, but when it did, I honored it as a real, life connection.

Levels of Learning

*F*or me, the levels of learning have always been interesting. This is the way they were taught to me.

Unconscious incompetence: you don't know you don't know.

Conscious incompetence: you know you don't know.

Conscious competence: you know but must put forth thoughtful effort to be competent.

Unconscious competence: you know without having to think about it.

I always found this to be a nifty little schema.

Subject-Verb Agreement

Beyond pronouns not agreeing with their antecedents, another common grammatical error is subject-verb agreement especially when prepositional phrases come into play. Often, the correct verb even "sounds wrong" because it immediately follows a prepositional phrase that is its opposite. I always encouraged my students to stay sharp and be sure to refer to the sentence's subject when selecting the verb.

Only Crazy People Think They Are Sane

I love this statement primarily because I am unsure to which camp I belong. If I am sane, then I will know I am crazy.

Teacher and T-Shirt

*H*ave you ever considered how much the word teacher sounds like t-shirt? I have. I also thought it may not be accidental. Teachers are basic, essential, come in all sizes, colors, and fit most any need or occasion. So if I didn't enunciate too well, and it sounded more like, "I am a t-shirt," when asked what I did, that was all right by me!

Why Time Seems to Go Faster As We Age

I distinctly remember our superintendent telling our class at the beginning of seventh grade that we would not believe how quickly junior high school (seventh and eighth grades) would go. He told us that we would be in ninth grade before we knew it. "Yeah, sure," we all thought. Much to our surprise, not only did the two years of junior high go quickly, but we were standing at the doorstep of our senior year dumb-founded, wondering where the time had gone.

While teaching, I would print a banner of the due dates of the Reading Log assignments for the entire year and hang it in my classroom for the second day of class. It extended 20' or more. The dates were in reverse order, so as each one passed I cut it off leaving the next due date at the end. I told my students when discussing it with them for the first time that they would be absolutely amazed at how quickly we would arrive at the final, May due date. They typically rolled their eyes with a "yeah, sure" attitude. About mid-April, they were beginning to see the truth of what I had told them, expressing how quickly the year had gone.

There is a mathematical explanation as to why time goes more quickly as we age. Each of the 365 days (a year) is a smaller percentage of our total existence. For example, for a five-year-old to wait until his or her next birthday, he or she has to wait twenty percent of his or her total existence. However, a fifty-year-old only has to wait two percent of his or her total existence. When a person gets to one hundred years, he or she only has to wait one percent of his or her total existence for the next birthday or if dementia has set in, it may seem like forever. Another factor, although not as precisely delineated, is that many/most times as we age, we become responsible for more than just ourselves; we have families. Taking the emphasis from ourselves and distributing it among others tends to add focal points resulting in less down time. There you have it.

"Education is a progressive response toward an increasingly subtler scale of values."

I love quotes with one of my very favorites being, *"Education is a progressive response toward an increasingly subtler scale of values."* My microbiology professor forty years ago at Michigan State University told us that in class one day. He mentioned who had said it, but today I only remember the quote. In fact, the professor told us, "If you don't remember anything else in this class, remember this quote." I took him at his word. When it came time for the final exam, I found myself questioning one of the last essay questions as to whether I really knew the answer he wanted. I had a couple of plausible ideas, but most certainly wasn't sure if either were correct. Well, I decided rather than choose in error, I would take him at his word, so I wrote, "I have a couple of ideas but I am not sure what the answer is; however, I do remember, *'Education is a progressive response toward an increasingly subtler scale of values.'*" I received full credit for the question, all of the twenty points. So, no wonder that quote has stayed with me.

The quote tells us that as we become educated, more informed, that we must change our thinking as things become less black and white, right or wrong. For example, when a child is young, not going near or touching the stove is desired. But as one grows, that's not a practical plan. (Well, it might be for me, since I don't like to cook.) There comes a time that we must learn to use the stove and observe good safety practices. It's no longer, "Don't touch it," but "Use it with care." Like so many things in life, when more information is known, the answers aren't so clear or easy.

Refreshed and Restored

*A*h... vacation! Yes, vacations were wonderful, but as the days passed, my thoughts turned back to school. I became anxious and invigorated to return to practice the craft I loved.

I sometimes wondered with our state's budget climate how long I would be able to continue teaching without jeopardizing my financial future. On this, I decided to not become anxious but rather trust the Universe. When proposals were offered, I consulted the Universe, weighed the options, and made a decision. After the state proposed its retirement incentive in the spring of 2010, I made a twelve-hour decision to retire. Many things called to me. After teaching thirty-eight years and absolutely loving it, it was time to try other things.

Combined Teacher Years

*W*hen I retired after teaching thirty-eight years, my family had a combined sixtieth birthday and retirement party honoring me, complete with caterer and professional photographer.

It was mid-July, so many of our friends were on vacation. Still, three hundred plus came that summer afternoon to celebrate with me. Of course, many attending were or had been teachers.

A few weeks after the party, I was having lunch with friends, and someone mentioned that at my party she had the thought that there sure were a lot of "teacher years" gathered there. Being a bit of a numbers nut, I decided to tally exactly how many "teacher years" were present at our home that Sunday afternoon in mid-July. While at it, and just for fun, I also counted the "school administration years" and "school secretarial years." **I tallied eighty-two school administration years, 150.4 school secretarial years, and 1,638.1 teacher years!** Wow!

The End

About the Author

Michele Hile is living on the family farm on which she was raised. After graduating from Michigan State University in 1972 and obtaining her teaching credentials, Michele accepted a teaching position with Caro Community Schools, her home school. She retired in June of 2010 after joyfully teaching thirty-eight years in the same system.

During her third year of teaching, she married her husband, Tom, who lived on his family's farm just a half mile north of her. Together, they farmed and raised two sons, John and Allen, who both now live in the greater Detroit area.

Michele genuinely enjoys people and is very active and community-oriented. She has been an ordained interfaith minister since 1997, serving those in need.

Ordering Information

In *My Journey of 55 Septembers ~ A Teacher's Story,* long-time educator, Michele Hile, shares her insights from her fifty-five years as a student and teacher, offering hope and encouragement, along with practical applications for teachers everywhere.

Copies of *My Journey of 55 Septembers ~ A Teacher's Story* are available for $20, or if shipping is required, $25.

Straw Walker Ink, LLC
1726 South Ringle Road
Caro, MI 48723
cen55375@centurytel.net
989-673-4332